MOSER'S
HOUR RECORDS

MOSER'S HOUR RECORDS

A HUMAN AND SCIENTIFIC ADVENTURE

FRANCESCO CONCONI

Vitesse Press
Brattleboro, Vermont

Translated by Patricia Ennis

This book first appeared in Italian as *I Segreti delle 'Ore' di Moser*, published by Compagnia Editoriale

ISBN 0-941950-26-3
Library of Congress card number 91-65026

Published by Vitesse Press
A division of FPL Corporation
28 Birge Street
Brattleboro, VT 05301-3206

Manufactured in the United States of America

Contents

About the hour record   vii

Preface   xi

1 The Mexico City records
     January 19 and 24, 1984   1

2 The sea-level records
     September 26 and October 3, 1986   15

3 The failures and Moscow and Vienna
     October 10 and 16, 1987   27

4 The Stuttgart record
     May 21, 1988   45

Photos from the record attempts   59

Graphs and tables   64

What is the Test Conconi?   77

About the author and the translator   81

About the hour record

World hour record—three words that define the ultimate test in cycling: one hour of near-maximal physical effort and intense concentration in an attempt to ride the greatest distance of any cyclist ever, to be the best in the world.

After months and even years of preparation, it all comes down to a rider, a bicycle, and a mercilessly ticking clock. Success in the hour record demands dedication, meticulous preparation, and the strongest of wills. That's what this book is about.

The time trial is often called the "race of truth," and for good reason. Gone are the variables that influence most bicycle races: the course, the other riders, the team strategies. The only opponents in the hour record attempt are time, the existing record, and one's self. (And sometimes, as we see in this account, that invisible enemy, the wind.)

The race for the hour record began nearly a century ago, in 1893, when Henri Desgrange rode 35.325 km in Paris. New records were set regularly through the turn of the century (all but one in Paris), until Oscar Egg rode 44.247 km in 1914. That record stood for nearly 20 years, until 1933, when another series of records began, culminating with Fausto Coppi's 45.871 km in 1942.

Coppi's record remained unbroken for 12 years until Jacques Anquetil crossed the 46-kilometer barrier in 1956, covering 46.159 km. Anquetil's record held for only 80 days before it was broken by Ercole Baldini, who in turn lost the record to Roger Riviere a year later. Riviere bettered his own record the following year (1958) and was the first man ever to surpass 47 km. His 47.347 km remained untouched until 1967, when Ferdinand Bracke rode 48.093.

Nearly a year later, Ole Ritter took the hour record to high altitude, covering 48.653 km in Mexico City in 1968. Until that time, all but one of the hour records (Denver, 1898) had been set at sea level (less than 600 meters altitude), and nearly all (18 out of 20) in Paris or Milan.

Four years later, in 1972, and again in Mexico City, Eddy Merckx set the famous 49.431-km limit that many observers believed to be unsurpassable. Unsuccessful attempts at the record by Ritter (48.880 km in 1974) and Hans Henrik Oersted (48.199 km in 1979) only served to reinforce the idea that Merckx's record was unbreakable. Then, in late 1983, someone else announced that he was going to try.

That someone was Francesco Moser, a 32-year-old Italian professional who was thinking about drawing the curtains on his great but declining cycling career. The idea of attempting the world hour record had occurred to Moser years earlier when, at age 23, he had accompanied Ritter to Mexico City and had seen the failed attempt to recapture the record from Merckx. Nine years later, having won two world championships (road and track), several national championships, three consecutive Paris-Roubaix races, three Baracchi Trophies, and numerous one-day classics, Moser still had the hour record on his mind.

But time was running out. Merckx had been 27 years old when he set the record that, by his own account, took 10 years off his life. Moser was already 32 when the 1983 cycling season drew to a close and he began thinking seriously about the hour record. The record attempt would not be easy, either financially or technically. He would need help from experts in various fields who believed in him and his abilities.

Fortunately, that help was available. Moser wasn't the only one who had been thinking about the world hour record. Dr. Enrico Arcelli of the Also company (makers of dietary products such as Enervit) had already discussed the possibility with Dr. Francesco Conconi, a professor of biochemistry. Conconi had developed a field test that had proven very useful in training runners and other athletes for endurance competition. Another interested party, in terms of sponsorship and advertising, was Paolo Sorbini, president of the Also Company.

So the stage was set for a human and scientific adventure. It began with a simple physical test and ended with five world hour records.

The man who developed that test, Dr. Francesco Conconi, is the one who tells the story, which begins on the dusty roads of his youth and ends on the slick surface of the indoor velodrome of Stuttgart, Germany. The story spans five years and seven countries. Most importantly, it's a success story that illustrates what science and human will together can achieve.

Patricia Ennis

Preface

"...but to pursue virtue and knowledge."
Dante, Inferno XXVI 120

I wrote this book to preserve and share the facts and emotions of the extraordinary experience I had with Francesco Moser. Cycling enthusiasts and experts will find here some of the training and racing data we collected, along with my comments on its physiological significance, which can also be applied to other endurance sports. But the story of Francesco Moser and his hour records transcends mere statistics. It's the story of a man in search of his own limits. Besides presenting the technical details, I wanted to reveal the human side of this athlete and the extremes of enthusiasm and disappointment, worry and joy that were interwoven with the conquest of his five records.

1
The Mexico City records
January 19 and 24, 1984

I can still remember the dusty roads of my youth when I raced bikes hoping to become a regional contender. In the years right after World War II and into the early '50s, the equipment we used and the training and racing conditions were primitive: unpaved roads, punctures, with spare tires slung over our shoulders. Wheel changes weren't allowed—if you flatted, you had to rip the tire off the rim, sometimes with your teeth. It was a big deal to have a Campagnolo rear derailleur with two levers on long rods: with one, you released the wheel; with the other, you moved the chain onto a different cog while pedaling backwards. Changing gears on a hard climb wasn't easy.

We confronted these external problems as they came along. They were part of the game, often an integral part, and they made the cycling adventure different than it is today. I say this somewhat regretfully.

Cycling isn't the only sport that has changed. Take mountain climbing, for example. The north face of the Matterhorn is much less of an adventure today than it was when Walter Bonatti scaled it in wintry solitude. Maybe this is because the route is known, or because of new kinds of mountaineering equipment and clothing, or maybe it's because of the different training and technique of today's climbers.

Or consider the marathon. It's not the grueling event it

once was if every year thousands of people finish this exhausting race without collapsing. Today's competitors know how to train, what to eat, what to wear, and what to do during the race. Yesterday's unknowns are gone.

Even competitive cycling has fewer mysteries, and rightly so. Cycling has become a combination of sport, entertainment, and business, all inseparably intertwined. Of course, it can still be tough and cruel—even today a rider sometimes has to be a hero, as he often did 50 years ago. But today, while a cyclist is an athlete above all, he's also a public figure and a businessman.

I've often asked myself, "What is adventure and what is its fascination?" The answer seems to be, "It's confronting the unknown."

Does this element still exist in modern sports? I think so, even if today there is less of the unknown in the world around us, which we know and can at least partially control. Rather, it's in the extraordinary mental and physical abilities demanded of the athlete, which sports help develop. In this respect, the modern athlete's adventure is similar to the research scientist's. They both continue to try new things, even at the risk of failure, spurred on by the desire to get new results.

This desire to know more was perhaps the principal motivation for Francesco Moser and me to try, to succeed, to fail, then to study and try again—through seven arduous attempts—to break the hour record.

The fascination of the hour

The cycling hour record is a special test, fascinating and involving—and not just to Italians or Europeans, who have always been cycling fanatics. Because cycling is so international, the results of this event are also appreciated in America, Australia, Japan, and China. In this sense, the hour record is similar in importance to world records in track and field.

Francesco Moser established five world hour records under three different environmental conditions: at 2,300 meters altitude (Mexico City, 1984, first 50.802 km and soon thereafter 51.151 km); at sea level on an outdoor velodrome (Milan, 1986, first 48.543 km and then 49.802 km); and finally at sea level on an indoor velodrome (Stuttgart, 1988, 50.644 km).

In each case, both for Moser and for those of us who worked with him, it was truly a race toward the unknown. We couldn't know if Francesco Moser had the necessary strength to beat Eddy Merckx or to repeat the record attempts within a short time. There was the factor of his age and whether the type of training developed for marathon runners would work for cyclists in general and for the hour record and Francesco in particular. Would tests that were suitable for monitoring training in other sports be useful in this specific case? And then, after the failed attempts in Moscow and Vienna, we didn't know whether Moser, by then 37, would be able to return to his peak.

But the adventure was exciting precisely because there were so many unknowns and so little apparent chance of success. It was like trying to scale a previously unconquered mountain peak—arduous but irresistible for anyone who falls under its spell.

Launching the attempt

Enrico Arcelli, a fellow sportsmedicine specialist, had been thinking about the hour record for some time and had discussed it with me a few years earlier. At that time we considered training a cyclist for the hour record by using the field test we had developed with Gian Paolo Lenzi to train marathon runners. Arcelli was thinking of making the attempt with Daniel Gisiger, a Swiss rider particularly good at time trialing.

I didn't hear any more about it until one day in September 1983, when Arcelli phoned me to talk about the hour record again. This time he suggested Francesco Moser. I pointed out that an expedition to Mexico would cost a lot of money, but Arcelli was sure he could count on the enthusiasm and financial support of Paolo Sorbini, owner of the Also company. He told me that a test done by Moser's trainer Aldo Sassi (on the track at Forli, I think) had produced ambiguous results, and he asked me to do one at Ferrara to see whether we thought Moser had the potential to break what nearly everyone believed to be the unbreakable 49.431-km record of Eddy Merckx.

The first test

I met Francesco Moser for the first time on September 30, 1983, at the Ferrara velodrome. It was a typical sultry late-summer afternoon, and a storm was threatening. As an *appassionato* of cycling, I knew Moser well by sight. I didn't know him personally, but his "aura" struck me immediately.

He listened attentively as I described how to perform the test at ever-increasing speeds. I told him how we had developed the test over several years as a means of evaluating the aerobic strength of athletes in various sports. He then put on the somewhat rudimentary heart rate monitor we were using at the time (a band around the chest connected by a wire to a small box that displayed the heart rate) and began to pedal. Though none of us knew it at the time, this was the first of innumerable tests he would do over the next five years.

Moser reached his anaerobic threshold at 46 kph—the best result among the cyclists we'd tested on the cement track at Ferrara. From our experience in other sports, we know that this "threshold" speed is approximately the speed an athlete can maintain during a one-hour effort. In short, it indicates optimal race pace for endurance events. One can go beyond this limit, but only by using emergency mechanisms, the kind activated during sprints or other short-term efforts.

Merckx's record

We studied the test results at length. Certainly they were far from the legendary performance of Eddy Merckx. However, the data, when examined closely, gave us a glimpse of undeveloped potential with considerable room for improvement. First of all, it was clear that Moser had developed the anaerobic capacity indispensable for the rapid changes of pace demanded by road racing, but which is not much use for the hour record. We believed specific training could reverse that situation. Moser's anaerobic threshold and his race pace could improve, though at the expense of his sprint.

Also, the Ferrara velodrome certainly wasn't one of the fastest: a smoother track would help close the gap on Merckx. So would the lower air resistance at 2,300 meters altitude in Mexico City. It seemed the 3,500 meters that separated Moser from the record could definitely be reduced. After having discussed these results with my longtime colleague, Dr. Michele Ferrari, I telephoned Milan to say that I believed Moser had substantial potential for improvement, enough to possibly break the hour record. But before launching the attempt, I thought it would be prudent for him to do a test run in Mexico. This would confirm how much advantage we could expect from the altitude and a better track. Moser and the sponsors agreed immediately.

The first trip to Mexico

Despite a long trip and a stopover in Madrid, the morning after we arrived in Mexico City we went right to work—first to the Olympic velodrome where Merckx had set his fantastic record 11 years earlier, then to the Mexican Olympic Sports Center velodrome. We wanted to compare tests and pick the track that would give us the best results. I personally preferred the velodrome Merckx used so Moser's record attempt would be directly comparable with the great Belgian champion's. But, unfortunately, the wooden surface of this track had been exposed to the elements for years and had deteriorated to the point of being practically useless. So we were forced to choose the 333-meter Olympic Sports Center velodrome—the site of all subsequent work and, finally, of the hour record. We decided to remedy the roughness of the cement with a layer of varnish in the zone of the track that Moser would ride.

Though we had some problems with unstable atmospheric conditions (the weather continued to be a thorn in my side for all of the outdoor record attempts), the tests we did during our short stay in Mexico City allowed us to verify repeatedly that at 2,300 meters Moser's anaerobic threshold rose to slightly more than 48 kph. Merckx's "lead" was already reduced to 1,200 meters.

It didn't take much to hypothesize that this gap could be narrowed further, given that there were other ways to get more improvement. For one thing, the time spent at high altitude could be extended to at least three weeks. In fact, I had already shown several times with marathon runners and race walkers, right there in Mexico City, that once the first few difficult days have passed, progressive improvements can be expected as the body adapts to the lower oxygen levels. Other improvements would come, at least theoretically, from specific hour-record training, which would reduce Francesco's sprint but at the same time increase his cruising speed.

And so, not only was Merckx closer than after the test at Ferrara, but we felt that Moser could gain on him considerably.

During our brief trip to Mexico City, Moser also tested different bicycles. By researching improved aerodynamics, we hoped to find mechanical ways to guarantee a higher speed for the same applied force.

We discussed and weighed the test results with Moser and were increasingly convinced that the idea of breaking the hour record was not absurd and that Francesco had the right stuff to do it.

Of course, the improvements we proposed were theoretical, verified in other sports with other athletes but not in cycling and not with Moser. Francesco, however, had no reservations. He was curious to find out whether training, tests, special bicycles, high altitude, and our theories would work or not. It was this Moser, always determined to go the limit, that I would come to know in the following years.

We returned to Italy after only five days, having decided to make the attempt. The meteorological information we were given in Mexico told us that the good weather usually turns into a rainy season at the end of January. So the attempt would have to be made in January 1984. Two months wasn't much time to prepare, but we thought we could do it, given Moser's already high level of conditioning.

Getting ready

We began the specific preparation in the beginning of December. Developing the physiological capabilities needed for the hour record wasn't the only problem. We also analyzed the many mechanical variables—frame, crankarms, handlebars, gearing, wheels. And the track had to be given an appropriate coating to make it smoother. Some of the short time available had to be devoted to the sponsors, who generously supported us but who also, for understandable business reasons, organized frequent press conferences with journalists who were torn between curiosity and skepticism.

Certainly the idea of breaking Merckx's record must have seemed very presumptuous. I made the mistake one day of saying, without enough explanation, that for me the record attempt was fun. It must have sounded as if I failed to take such a historic undertaking seriously (especially to journalist Mario Fossati, who justifiably reprimanded me in *La Repubblica*). I was referring to the fact that the applied research I had begun with Moser, with its uncertainties and its many problems, was very exciting for me. It was full of scientific possibilities, and it involved a sport I had participated in as a boy and still loved.

"What is this, a funeral?"

One of my clearest memories of this period is of the first training session at the Milan sports palace. One of the key ways to improve the anaerobic threshold is to have the athlete train at race pace, which is usually far below his maximum. This results in relatively boring intervals that last for some minutes and are repeated several times during each training session. Moser's mechanic, Fucacci, and masseur, Gamberini, who evidently were expecting killer workouts, came up to me and asked, bewildered, "What is this, a funeral?" No, it was simply anaerobic threshold training, a technique that had been used on runners for a few years with good results. Who knew whether it would work with Moser?

Aldo Sassi followed the daily progress of Moser's training program, which included, among other things, uphill strength training—pushing big gears at a low cadence on hills with grades of up to 10 percent. We did this to increase Moser's muscle power, although I'm not sure now that this type of workout is beneficial for the hour record. I must say, however, that Moser always included it willingly in his training and felt good about doing it.

There was a lot to do and time seemed to be running short. Many people were involved in the preparations: doctors, researchers, mechanics, sponsors, and journalists. Everyone had his duties. Some were working on the lenticular wheel, others were working on the frame at the Moser brothers' workshop in Gardolo.

Moser was concentrating on his objective. I came to appreciate his clarity in deciding what to do and what not to do. He's not the type you can force things on. He wanted to know about each procedure and the reason for it, and then he would decide what seemed reasonable. Not that he didn't listen to advice—he just didn't accept it passively.

After a month of very intense work, Moser and his entourage finally left for Mexico for three weeks of acclimatization at altitude. It was December 29, 1983.

Mexico City

At the beginning of the training period in Mexico City, Michele Ferrari, who had gone with the group to Mexico, phoned me almost daily about how things were going. At first everything went fairly well. Moser's threshold was between 48.5 and 49 kph. The track surface had been coated and was smooth, according to both Francesco's subjective impressions and our test results.

Then things began to go less well: Moser had some problems adapting to the altitude. There is usually a significant drop in performance after about a week of altitude training, and though this was expected, when it happened to Francesco it was disturbing. But with every passing day the results of the tests and the trials at race pace improved steadily. On January 6, after some bad weather fortunately forced him to rest a bit, Moser covered 46.4 km in one hour with moderate effort. After that the telephone calls from Mexico were less worried (and less worrying).

When I finally freed myself from my duties at the university and joined the group in mid January, Moser's test results were already very high. Ferrari, who unfortunately had to return home when I got there, met me at the Mexico City airport and told me about a very encouraging training session Moser had had that same day: three 10-km trials at a pace of about 50 kph. Even more importantly, the effort had seemed relatively easy, not maximal, and Moser still had some energy reserves when the trials were over. Of course, the hour record was another matter, but that kind of a performance can only come from an athlete in excellent physical condition.

I never tried to contradict those who were skeptical about the record attempt. If I hadn't had the information I did, even I would have had doubts. Despite the results of the field tests, I couldn't be sure that all would go well. Who could have guaranteed that the test results would carry over to the hour record itself, given that we had no actual experience in that regard? The skeptics were right in considering Merckx's record to be practically unassailable. Today, some 16 years later, only one athlete besides Moser has done better than Merckx—Soviet rider Viatcheslav Ekimov. In fact, we should thank those who said, "He'll never do it." It's partly because of their skepticism that Moser's record came to be fully appreciated.

Lenticular wheels

A few days before the record attempt the lenticular wheels arrived in Mexico. There had been problems and a lot of discussion about the wheels—and their patent—from the design stage on. Over time, however, we confirmed what the first tests had indicated: these wheels offered a definite advantage, especially under calm atmospheric conditions, but not enough to change the results substantially.

I'll take this opportunity to say that others may have already thought of disk wheels. Even before the record attempt, there was talk of disk wheels, and pictures of them appeared in cycling magazines. But that matters little. Just as other explorers went to America before Columbus, but the discovery of the New World is certainly attributable to him, many others may have thought about lenticular wheels before Moser, but it was he, with the two records in Mexico, who "discovered" and conclusively applied them.

The countdown

We had reached the countdown. Our tension inevitably mounted. The first journalists arrived.

Fortunately, because of his prolonged training at altitude, Moser continued to improve. Finally, he was ready. We decided to move up the record attempt to the morning of January 19, without waiting for the fans to arrive, because the atmospheric conditions, which were crucial, were predicted to be favorable then.

We were thinking about a race pace of approximately 50 kph, which was prudent considering the test data, and we officially aimed for the 20 km record. We would continue to the end of the hour if things went well. But I think that everyone, or almost everyone, headed for the velodrome on that bright January morning thinking about the hour record. No one joked or talked sarcastically about the attempt. This athlete, who was about to try to defeat the unbeatable Merckx and undergo the terrible effort that the hour record requires, had surely earned the respect, if not the confidence, of everyone there.

The first record

Francesco warmed up, first by himself, then behind the motorcycle. We did a couple of tests, and then Moser went into the dressing room to put on the black skinsuit that came to identify images of his first record.

In the minutes before the start, Francesco was the only person who was calm and focused. We made some final checks on his bicycle, his shoes, and other clothing. Finally, amidst a noticeable widespread tension, the hour record attempt began.

It took only a few laps to discover that Moser could maintain a pace well above 50 kph without maximal effort. We could see it in the way he pedaled easily, in the fact that he wasn't sitting on the tip of his saddle, and in his facial expression—tense but not suffering. Moser surpassed the world record for 5 km (of Hans-Henrik Oersted) and for 10 and 20 km (held by Merckx). His advantage over Merckx was 14 seconds at 10 km, 36 seconds (equivalent to 500 meters) at 20 km, and increased significantly with each passing minute.

Considering the exciting progress of the record attempt to that point, there was no question of interrupting it after 20 km. Moser held out, and how! His effort wasn't ideally distributed over the 60 minutes, though. He started too fast, and his pace suffered some ups and downs, with low points of 49 kph and high points of 52-53 kph. I think these variations were signs of insufficient concentration, although an occasional wind was partly responsible.

Did we underestimate the difficulty of this undertaking? Perhaps. Every so often Moser lost his concentration and his speed dropped, much to our concern. But when we alerted him to the fact, he increased his speed immediately, showing that he still had energy reserves. In one hour Francesco covered, with relative ease, 50.802 km—1,371 meters more than the previous record. He would have lapped Merckx four times.

Everyone was euphoric once the record was established. Certainly, we had thought Moser could beat Merckx's record, but never by so much. News of the record astonished and excited everyone: photographs of Moser during his great effort appeared on the front pages of many newspapers, even those not devoted to sports. Congratulations and praise came from all over the world for this nearly 34-year-old athlete from Trent—a man who emerged victorious from an "impossible" challenge.

"Moser, un record dehors du temps" read the headline in *L'Equipe*, the prestigious French sports journal. ("Moser, a record outside of time.") Even French president Mitterand sent his congratulations. It was the kind of reception the world reserves for the setting of great records, such as the four-minute mile of Roger Bannister at Oxford, England, in 1954. People were stunned not only by the fact that someone had outdone the unbeatable Merckx, but also that a man on a bike had traveled more than 50 km in one hour.

Moser's freshness after the record, an effort that had nearly killed others in the past, astonished people too. Merckx, for example, was so exhausted after setting his record that he said, "I will never do anything like that again." Moser, on the other hand, announced that he intended to repeat the record attempt within a few days.

What was behind this decision, one which most people considered risky and even dangerous physically? First of all, the initial attempt left a certain bitter taste in our mouths: the ease with which Moser set the new record showed that he hadn't used his full potential. Francesco knew he hadn't given it his all and, understandably, wanted a second chance to perform at his maximal level. He didn't want to leave things undone. Also, he didn't want to make it too easy for someone to break his record in the future.

And there was the problem of Moser's many fans, who arrived in Mexico only to discover that the record attempt had already been made. Naturally, they were happy about the record, but still, they had wanted to be there when it happened. Francesco didn't want to disappoint those fans who came expressly to cheer him on. So, without much hesitation, he decided to make a second attempt.

The second record

The first attempt had in fact cost Moser very little. The tests performed during the succeeding days indicated a rapid recovery. We planned to make the second attempt on Monday, January 23, four days after the first. We knew another day or two of recovery would have been better, but the weather reports predicted rain, which didn't allow us much time. Also, Monday is a good day in Mexico City: the factories are closed on Sunday, and the smog that usually hangs over the city is not as thick as later in the week.

This time there were lots of spectators. The morning was cold. At 8:30 a.m., on the shady, eastern curve of the track, it was only 6 degrees Celsius (43 degrees Fahrenheit), forcing us to wait at least two hours for the temperature to reach an acceptable level. Meanwhile, the fans were showing signs of impatience. We even heard an occasional hiss. But we couldn't make a record attempt under those conditions. Air resistance is definitely greater when it's cold. (It increases approximately 1 percent for every drop of three degrees Celsius in this temperature range.)

Moser had a hard time warming up, and the first tests yielded poor results. But slowly he began to find his rhythm, and the umpteenth test showed he was ready.

It was nearly 11 a.m. when he finally took off. Our schedule called for a race pace of slightly more than 51 kph, but Moser went above that immediately. His average speed for the first 5 km was 51.850 kph—despite the seconds lost to the standing start, a new record (5:47.16) The speed was a bit too fast, however, and Francesco was forced to slow down. Also, an annoying wind came up, and he had to work very hard to maintain his speed. Despite the wind, Francesco managed to set a new record at 20 km as well (23:21.59, average speed 51.370 kph). We hoped the wind would die down, but it continued to blow, causing almost unbearable fatigue.

It was here that I witnessed a Moser I was just beginning to know. He could have given up at that point—the hour record was his and his fans had just seen him set two other world records. Instead, he pushed himself to the limit for the rest of the hour. Even during the slowest 5 km, Moser maintained a speed greater than that of his preceding record. The changes in speed this time were not the result of an uneven effort, but rather were due to changes in wind speed. This time, he suffered great fatigue.

At the end of the hour, Francesco had covered the now-famous 51.151 km.

How far would he have gone that day under ideal atmospheric conditions? 52 km? Perhaps. However, sports aren't based on "what ifs" and "buts." Results are what count. And we were lucky: the next day the weather changed, and an unusually strong wind swept the Mexico City plateau. In all probability, we set the second hour record on the last possible day.

News of the two hour records traveled around the world. Moser became the symbol of research applied to sports. Many attributed his results primarily to science. Certainly scientific research helped but, to quote Moser, "It doesn't make a race horse out of an ass." He was perfectly right. In my opinion, the two records came about, for the most part, because of Moser's extraordinary physical and mental capacities.

2
The sea-level records September 26 and October 3, 1986

After the great successes in Mexico City, Michele Ferrari and I, along with other colleagues at the University of Ferrara, followed Moser's road racing career. We saw him win the Tour of Italy and other important races. But we also saw him lose some of his motivation and the desire to continue training as diligently and intensely as needed to stay at the highest competitive level. Yet Moser's loss of motivation wasn't surprising. Like every other sport practiced for a long time, cycling can become a series of dull and repetitive exercises.

In the spring of 1986 we found ourselves talking about the idea of attempting the hour record at sea level. (This wasn't an entirely new project. In fact, Francesco had mentioned the possibility immediately after the Mexico City records.) The idea arose partly from the fact that there had been a number of other attempts at the hour record recently, and they had attracted considerable publicity. Moser, no longer stimulated by his usual cycling activity, wanted a way to relive the electrifying experiences of Mexico. And he knew he had athletic potential not yet fully exploited.

Announcing the sea-level attempt

When we announced our decision to try the hour record at sea level, no one showed the skepticism that had accompanied the altitude record three years earlier, but no one showed much interest either.

To add to the Mexico records would be no small undertaking. The effort was likely to result in an event that would be appreciated on a technical level, but one that would be less than exciting as a sports spectacle. I even thought there might be more to lose than gain, both in image and results. To succeed would require an outstanding performance, one that would invite comparison with the altitude records. (Could Moser still do it?) Furthermore, Francesco would have to prove again that he had those Pied Piper qualities that had guaranteed people's interest and enthusiasm in the past. This was a sticky problem, given that the road racing season was in full swing, which distracted Francesco and also detracted attention from the sea-level record attempt, planned for fall.

Still, the record attempt slowly took shape. In the spring it seemed far away, but with the passing months we began to feel that we had too little time. It was like studying for a test at the last minute.

This time we had to break the record of Hans-Henrik Oersted, the Dane who had covered 48.145 km the year before at Bassano del Grappa. Oersted had surpassed, by only a few meters, a record set years earlier at the Olympic velodrome in Rome by Ferdinand Bracke, a great time trialist and a Belgian like Merckx. Oersted was a middle-distance rider, less adapted to short or long distances.

It should be noted that Oersted's ride at Bassano was impeded by a strong wind during the second half-hour. He probably could have done even better under more favorable conditions. At the altitude of Mexico City, his effort would have been worth approximately 50 km. Although it wasn't an easy record to break, we thought Moser could do it. The problem was not so much to break the Dane's record as it was to get a distance that would withstand comparison with the Mexico record and so would not detract from Moser's prestige.

We decided that Moser had to surpass 49 km in one hour. Since the difference in performance between sea level and the 2,300-meter altitude of Mexico City accounts for approximately 2 km, it was clear that Moser had to be in the same great condition of three years earlier if we were to get good results. As the date for the record attempt approached, these considerations became worries.

Training for the attempt

We thought it would be a good idea to combine preparation for the new record attempt with the world road championships taking place that year in Colorado Springs, Colorado, at an altitude of 2,000 meters. We wanted Moser to train at altitude so he would be in top shape at sea level. The altitude training wasn't limited to Moser's stay in the U.S., however. Before going to Colorado, he trained at 2,050 meters at the Fedaia Pass on Mount Marmolada in Italy.

In the U.S. Moser pedaled well at a steady pace. I was there too, for an international sportsmedicine congress. Professional team director Alfredo Martini told me he was impressed by Moser's pace on a long climb that rose to about 4,000 meters. This was a good omen for the hour record but not necessarily good for a race like the world road championships in which the ability to change pace frequently is more important than being able to maintain a constant high pace. This ability to change pace was characteristic of Moreno Argentin, who won the professional world road championship at Colorado in a beautiful race.

Upon returning to Italy, we had 20 days to reaccustom Moser to track riding and to the different saddle position. We had to reorient his training to the steady pace of the hour record, and to experiment with wheels and other bike parts that had evolved in shape, weight, and rigidity in the three years since Mexico. We studied velodromes closely and finally selected the Vigorelli, which is more protected from the wind than the one in Bassano.

The atmosphere in Milan was quieter than in Mexico, with fewer people and less tension. We stayed at a friend's house, and Francesco was surrounded by people close to him: his wife Carla, his children Francesca and Carlo, his brother Enzo, his doctor Michele Ferrari, his masseur Giorgio Gamberini, and Giorgio's wife Anna, who is an excellent cook.

Everything went well: the test results and Moser's race pace rose progressively to optimal levels as the effects of altitude training became apparent. Moser's training also benefitted from the Baracchi Trophy, a two-man time trial he rode with Didi Thurau. Thurau is a West German athlete of great class; however, toward the finish he was unable to maintain the impressive pace set by Moser, who was then approaching his peak condition.

The public and the media began to show a growing interest in the sea-level attempt. How could one not get excited about a record attempt by Francesco Moser—an athlete loved by so many—especially when the event was set against the background of the Vigorelli velodrome, the colorful scene of many earlier records? Certainly the TV and newspapers did a lot to publicize the record attempt, but I don't believe they could have attracted the same attention with any other athlete.

Milan

We set Friday, September 26, as the date for the attempt, taking the television coverage into account. Autumn in Lombardy, with its soft colors and morning mists, isn't rainy, but unfortunately it's a bit windy in the afternoon. So Friday evening, along with a crowd such as hadn't been seen for years at the Vigorelli, we had that unwelcome companion of the hour record—the wind. The mountains were some distance away, and there were houses around the track, but the troublesome wind arrived just the same.

Perhaps it would be helpful to explain why this is such a

problem. The primary effort a cyclist puts out is overcoming air resistance. Pedaling at 20 kph against a wind that's blowing 10 kph requires almost as much effort as pedaling at 30 kph with no wind. And if the cycling speed is 50 kph and the wind is 10 kph, the effort required is about equal to that of riding at 60 kph. It's true that on a track one does laps, riding partly against the wind and partly with it. But the fatigue that accumulates while riding against the wind has a negative effect on the athlete's overall performance. The cyclist ends up going slower than he otherwise might, even when riding with the wind. This is why calm atmospheric conditions are necessary to set outdoor records. It's also why indoor record attempts are preferable.

Given the windy conditions, we knew it would be better to postpone the attempt because the outcome would not be proportional to the effort. But that was easier said than done. There were all the people who had come to watch, as well as those all over the world who had already turned on their TVs. These were the thoughts that crossed our minds before the start. Francesco was a little more tense than usual, and no wonder.

"After five o'clock, the wind usually dies down," we told ourselves, hoping that the pattern of the preceding days would repeat itself. But it didn't happen that day.

Moser started anyway. "If you see that it's not going well, make me stop," he said to me just before the start.

Terrible fatigue

The gun fired and he was on his way. The 49-kph pace we had proposed was immediately impossible to maintain. The wind gauge registered gusts of up to 30 kph, and we knew Francesco must work like never before or he would slow down. It was an ordeal. I wanted to stop him after only a few minutes, but I didn't, still hoping that the wind would die down. No such luck—the conditions didn't change.

"Stop him!" I repeated to myself. But his average speed continued to exceed 48.5 kph, higher than Oersted's record. How can you stop an athlete who's winning?

Time passed. At the half-hour, his accumulated fatigue was already so great that, even if we interrupted the attempt, he wouldn't be able to repeat it the next day, even with good atmospheric conditions. I could see how much Francesco suffered, and I suffered too, but by then there was nothing to do but continue.

At about 40 minutes, the wind died down a bit. Immediately his average speed, which had dropped to 48.4 kph, went up again, indicating that despite the terrible effort, Francesco hadn't yet spent all his reserves. He finished at 48.543 km, a new hour record at sea level.

Moser suffered cramps in both legs, which shocked the spectators and the photographers more than it did us. The cramps were in muscle groups that cyclists usually don't use much and resulted from the effort expended in the unusual riding position he'd had to adopt. Overall, his condition was great: he was completely lucid, and his cardiovascular system immediately returned to normal. But the fatigue he suffered this time was incredible.

"I believe that I suffered more than Merckx did in Mexico City," he said in an interview.

"Moser: the record of the heart," declared the headline in a sports daily. Personally, I was anything but satisfied. First of all, the result was decidedly below the estimated 49 km I was sure Francesco would have surpassed under normal conditions. Plus, he had put out all that effort to go only 398 meters further than Oersted. Once again I was disturbed by the fact that weather conditions could affect the results so strongly. For the first time I began to think of a record attempt free from such atmospheric variations, on an indoor velodrome where this great athlete could express his real potential.

A new attempt

Moser, Ferrari, and I dined together at the Tre Pini restaurant and reconsidered what had been, in our opinion, only a partial success. "With the same effort and no wind, what would the outcome have been?" we asked ourselves.

"How about if we try again next week?" I blurted out, almost as a joke.

Francesco didn't say no. It was Saturday evening; the next day he would compete in a circuit race. ("What courage," I said to myself, given the cramps that he suffered a short time ago.) "Let's talk about it Monday morning," Moser said, as I left for home.

On Monday morning our impulse was, indeed, to try again. But at that point the decision was not definite, much less official. We told ourselves, "Let's see how things go this week. Then, on Thursday, we'll decide what to do."

Moser was having terrible leg pains, a consequence of the cramps, and the pains were diminishing so slowly we couldn't prepare as we wanted. Roberto Rossetti, a physical therapist from our university group, worked on Moser's leg muscles at length, relieving most of the small muscular contractions. But the troubles weren't over yet: the next morning the leg pains were greatly reduced, but the usual tests yielded discouraging results, to say the least. We simply were not ready.

Michele phoned me at Ferrara and told me he thought we should forget the whole thing. Being an eternal optimist, I didn't want to accept defeat. I suggested the possibility that the muscle relaxant Moser had taken the evening before may not have completely passed through his system and may have negatively affected his performance.

"Let's wait until tonight," I said. "Then we'll conduct some more tests and make a decision based on the results."

I was lucky. That very evening things started to go better. The next day the test results were considerably better, and by evening they had reached optimal levels. The muscle relaxant had been eliminated by Moser's body; now he was truly well. The leg pains had disappeared, and our tests yielded the highest results Moser had ever attained at sea level. He was ready to try again.

The fourth record

The experience of the preceding week was still vivid, and I was anxious about what the atmospheric conditions would be on the day and hour of the record attempt. I studied every weather bulletin apprehensively. It became a kind of obsession for me. It was like students at exam time—the ones who have studied a lot are often the most worried because they fear some unexpected question will spoil months of preparation. Similarly, I didn't want bad weather to keep Francesco from harvesting the fruits of his work and his abilities.

Instead, we were truly fortunate: the conditions on the evening of October 3 were perfect. We studied the results of a test performed shortly before the start with Moser, who by then knew how to interpret the tests himself. His results were even better than on preceding days.

There was a big crowd. "Moser is like good wine. The older he gets, the better he gets," read a banner made by some of his faithful fans.

As the attempt began, every problem got resolved and every worry disappeared. Not only was Moser completely recovered from the previous week's ride, but, according to the results, that week probably served as excellent training. His scheduled race pace, which we knew from the tests to be easily within reach, was slightly more than 49 kph. But with his first pedal strokes, Moser went up to almost 50 kph. Deep down, however, he didn't believe the messages his body was sending him and prudently slowed down during the first half-hour, wary of the times we were relaying to him.

At the half-hour point, Moser felt sure he could maintain a faster pace. So in the second half of the attempt, just when most athletes feel the effects of the effort and are forced to slow down, Francesco picked up his pace. In that second half-hour, he covered slightly less than 25 km, and the average speed for the final 5 km was 50.550 kph. Moser gave the distinct impression of being able to cover 50 km, which is a tremendous feat at sea level.

The final result was 49.802 km—371 meters more than Merckx at altitude. Thirty years earlier Jacques Anquetil had ridden 46.159 km on this same track; Moser had a 4:23 advantage on the Frenchman at that distance.

Evaluation and regret

Moser's performance had been incredible. It demonstrated strength, ease, and consistency but also, unfortunately, some untapped potential. Once again there was regret—his and ours. A more evenly distributed effort and a slightly larger gear (we had used one appropriate for 49 kph, not 50) would have given him an even better result—50 km at sea level. Part of his power had been lost in spinning his legs too fast, using a gear suitable for a slower speed. Given the results of the test we did before the start (more than 51 kph at his anaerobic threshold), we could, and perhaps should, have dared to use the larger gear. It was like failing to reach top speed in a car, not for lack of power in the engine but for lack of a fifth gear.

I returned home pondering the data from this extraordinary performance: the Moser of Milan would probably have covered 52 km in Mexico City!

Another thing that bothered me considerably and that I thought about in the days following the ''almost 50'' of Milan was the fact that Moser still hadn't attempted a record under truly standard conditions—that is, indoors and without the affect of atmospheric changes. A record attempt under such conditions would provide a definitive statement of Moser's athletic worth and would lend a sense of completeness to our story of the hour record from a technical standpoint as well.

My thought surprised me: ''Who knows what distance Moser could cover at the velodrome in Moscow?'' I had been told it was extremely smooth. I commented in a newspaper on Moser's results at the Vigorelli:

''Next year Francesco will retire from bicycle racing. But this isn't to say that before retiring he won't try to break the one hour record he still lacks—on an indoor track.

Because it's not influenced by atmospheric factors, that record would guarantee standard conditions and make it possible to compare various performances.

"The four experiences I've had with Moser have been fantastic, on both human and scientific levels. And Francesco is still researching his limits. I hope to be present for a fifth time."

News from Moscow

A few days later, as if by fate, the newspapers published a brief item that excited our interest, our curiosity, and our admiration: Soviet amateur Viatcheslav Ekimov had ridden 49.672 km in one hour on the Moscow velodrome, only 130 meters less than Moser rode at Milan.

If this result had come a month earlier, we would have modified our plans and objectives for the Vigorelli record. Let's be honest. Ekimov's ride would certainly have worried us. And if we had heard about it after our first record, after so much suffering for a result so inferior to the Soviet's, we would have been discouraged and might not have repeated the attempt.

Fortunately, Ekimov's result came after Milan. And so, without knowing it, Ekimov challenged Moser—a challenge that was accepted immediately. I must confess, both Francesco and I underestimated the Soviet's result. I said to Moser, "If you rode 49.802 km outdoors, it'll be easy for you to do even better indoors under more favorable conditions, even better than Ekimov." Francesco agreed.

The record set at Milan convinced us that, under ideal conditions (without wind), on a good indoor velodrome, Moser could close his account with the hour record by exceeding 50 km at sea level. The idea that "one could do better" very much influenced both Moser and me. I was always wanting to get results that could be compared with other athletes' results, something that's only possible when there are standard conditions. And also, we wanted to tackle the indoor record simply because we were challenged by Ekimov's result.

As I tell this story, it sounds as if we were sure that all we had to do was go to the track and do it. This, in fact, was our conviction (and our mistake): the indoor record seemed easy to us. Consequently, we confronted it with a certain overconfidence, without the necessary caution and determination.

The first trip to Moscow

Many people thought the Olympic velodrome in Moscow was ideal for this attempt, especially after Ekimov's exceptional result. We decided to inspect the track in early July 1987. Traveling in the Soviet Union wasn't easy. We had to overcome many bureaucratic problems, both in Italy and in Moscow, to be able to collect the necessary information in the short time available. Francesco and I went to Moscow alone, but we were helped with our various problems by Soviet and Italian sports people who frequented an Italian restaurant at the Hotel Mezdunarodnaja. Some of them even helped record the times at the track, which was indeed very smooth and beautiful.

The test results during our three-day stay were quite good, and Francesco was feeling positive. Returning to Milan on July 9, we had no doubts: we would go to Moscow in October for Moser's final record.

3
The failures at Moscow and Vienna October 10 and 16, 1987

Moser continued the 1987 road racing season, but for him it was a season without notable results or competitive drive. He crashed while training just before the Tour of Italy, was injured, and had to forfeit the race. Once he recovered, he rode some good races, such as the Tour of the Apennines, but without the brilliance of an athlete at his peak. His performance at the world championships at Villach, Austria, was also less than spectacular.

Finally, around September 10, we started training for the record. We had one month's time—not much, but enough, or so we thought. After all, Francesco was not beginning at zero; he had continued to train and race on the road. This time, unlike the year before for the Vigorelli records, we decided that training at altitude was unnecessary. Training on the track would be the basic preparation, mostly at the velodromes in Milan and Bassano del Grappa. Moser rode in the Baracchi Trophy in mid September, once again with a time trial partner who was unable to maintain the pace, Jesper Worre of Denmark.

On September 26, we went to Stuttgart, West Germany, for testing on an indoor velodrome similar to the one we'd use in Moscow two weeks later. In addition to the usual anaerobic threshold tests using various equipment,

Francesco rode some half-hour trials at race pace. He did 86 laps (24.571 km) in 30:15.16, for an average speed of 48.731 kph. Our impression was that he rode with relative ease, even increasing his pace toward the end. Certainly he had to work to attain 50 kph, but we were satisfied with the test results.

For one thing, the track in Stuttgart was not as smooth as the one in Moscow. Secondly, Moser had been training hard for the past few weeks—his performance would inevitably improve as soon as he tapered his workload. Moreover, we had another two weeks for specific training and further improvement. And the effort put forth in a simulated race, such as the half-hour trial, is never the same as the real event. In short, we found a hundred reasons to convince ourselves that we were on the road to success.

Uncertainty

We arrived in Moscow a week before the attempt. In addition to Francesco's wife Carla, his brother Enzo, Dr. Ferrari, and Giorgio Gamberini, others joined the caravan: Gian Luigi Stanga and Natale Maderna, Fulvio Astori (who coordinated an efficient press service), journalists, and a television crew. Shortly thereafter Francesco's brother Aldo and many of Moser's fans arrived, taking advantage of the opportunity to visit Leningrad and Moscow.

The tests told us that Moser had improved his condition since Stuttgart. His anaerobic threshold was very high—his engine was as powerful as ever. However, on Tuesday, October 6, when Moser did his last hard training (10 km at race pace, three times) I got the impression that, even though he managed to ride at 50 kph, it cost him more than it should have. He started out fast but, surprisingly, had trouble maintaining the pace. I began to wonder about his endurance, even though he had worked on it more that year, taking longer training rides than before the other record attempts. Furthermore, his road training and racing had continued until just a few weeks earlier. I didn't know what was wrong. I was concerned, but I didn't show it.

Meanwhile, the international sports world focused its attention on this ambitious attempt—50 km in one hour by a man no longer young and at the end of his career.

The Moscow attempt

Friday, October 10, was the day of truth. After Francesco warmed up, we ran the usual preliminary tests. The results, however, were not usual: both the base and the maximal heart rates were much higher than expected. In fact, they were the highest we had ever recorded for Moser. Even so, the data didn't convince me. I maintained that this was a sign of emotional tension, of unusual stress.

Perhaps subconsciously Francesco felt he was unprepared to give his final performance on an internationally televised stage. Perhaps he was afraid he wouldn't fulfill the expectations of the many spectators who had rushed there to cheer him on, or the international experts on the sidelines. Maybe the annoyance of having to coordinate the start with the TV broadcast played a role. Finally, and this was something we discovered only later, the temperature of the velodrome had been set too high and that may have increased the demands on Moser's cardiovascular system. However, there was no alternative but to start at the scheduled time.

The pitiless diagnosis came immediately. After some exciting and overly fast initial laps, Moser slowed to less than 50 kph. He persisted desperately until about 12 minutes had passed, but he just wasn't up to the task. He was forced to slow progressively, to 49, 48, and even 47 kph approaching the 40-minute mark, amidst the painful silence of his fans and our support crew. The satisfaction felt by some of Ekimov's fans was evident and very disturbing. There was even some hissing.

But Francesco was a professional who played his part with dignity, giving it his all as the end of the hour neared. He covered 48.637 km, 1,035 meters less than Ekimov, and much less than the 50 km that had seemed a relatively easy goal to attain after the Milan record the year before. It was a bitter failure, and I couldn't understand it.

We returned home disconcerted and incredulous. Weighing the pros and cons, we decided to try again a week later. Moser had performed better the second time around in both Mexico and Milan. We would see whether or not the attempt in Moscow had been good training. We would make sure the indoor air temperature wasn't so high.

Should we go back to the Soviet Union? Some wanted to; the Moscow track really was fast. But it was too difficult to organize another trip to Moscow. We decided to try Vienna, closer and easier to reach, even though the Vienna track was shorter and therefore harder to ride than the one in Moscow.

The Vienna attempt

Once more, the organizational machine was quickly put in motion, and two days later we were together again—technicians, fans, television crew, and publicists. Francesco really knew how to get people involved, how to make them respond on any occasion, even a less than favorable one like this.

The inevitable tests showed that Francesco had increased his strength slightly since Moscow. But strength wasn't the problem. In Moscow he had lacked endurance, as shown by the way his speed dropped with the passing minutes. In Vienna on October 16 Moser was a bit faster: at 10 km he was 6 seconds ahead of his Moscow time, and at 20 km he had gained 18 seconds. But the basic problem, the progressive slowing of his race pace, was unchanged. The graphs of both the Moscow and Vienna attempts revealed the same pattern. A comparison of those graphs with the ones from Mexico and Milan showed that the endurance problem was a new one.

In the Vienna attempt, the small computers we used to follow Moser's progress projected a final distance of about 49 km. This was better than the week before but well below our objective—the 49.672 km covered by Ekimov. There was no reason to continue, and at the 27th minute I reluctantly called a halt to the attempt.

What went wrong?

During the return trip from Vienna, I thought about what might have caused this double failure, and I discussed it with Michele Ferrari (who made a grim diagnosis: old age) and with Gianni Marchesini, our occasional traveling companion. One thing was clear: in Moscow and Vienna, Moser had used only part of his strength—48-49 kph instead of the 50-51 kph of which he was capable. His start was appropriate to his potential, but after a short while, for some unknown reason, he had to slow down quite a bit to be able to continue. The reason for this failing strength eluded me.

After the negative results were confirmed in Vienna there was an air of demobilization. Moser's cycling career seemed definitely over—unfortunately without the hour record that had seemed so easy to us and that we had thought of as a well-deserved conclusion.

There was one final road event in the season, the Firenze-Pistoia time trial on October 24, a week after the second unsuccessful record attempt. This race struck me as a good opportunity to complete the study of this negative period, if only for conclusive confirmation, and perhaps to find some answers to the questions that tormented me and to the hypotheses I was formulating.

I proposed to Francesco that he record his heart rate during the race and submit to blood sampling before and after. He willingly agreed. To my surprise, he was still curious, even though what was done was done and whatever information we gathered would seem to serve little purpose. I was amazed by his willingness to continue this tiring and unrewarding effort, especially considering that the disappointment of his recent failures must have still been painful. This persistence was undoubtedly one of Francesco's special attributes. It led him to attempt the impossible, beating Merckx's record, and to keep going when it would have seemed more reasonable to quit once and for all. It was a lesson of life: this is how you get results!

Firenze-Pistoia

I followed the race in a car, and we measured times and speeds, kilometer by kilometer. At the end we drew the umpteenth graph. Once again, the data from Moscow and Vienna was confirmed. If Francesco dared to go over 50 kph, he immediately had to slow to 47-48 kph, and it took 7 or 8 minutes each time for him to resume a speed he could maintain, about 49 kph. At this speed he was working at a submaximal level. His heart rate was less than 170 beats per minute. The heart rate he could reach during a prolonged effort like a time trial was definitely higher. In short, the obstacle didn't seem to be his heart, of which he was asking a submaximal effort, but his muscles, which were unable to maintain 50 kph.

Data collected previously for both running and cycling showed that an athlete can sustain a speed for a long time if it's slightly lower than his threshold as evaluated by the Test Conconi. In contrast, speeds above the threshold can only be maintained for brief periods—the athlete has to slow down because of lactic acid build-up. Lately, and for the first time since we began working with Moser, the test data and the race results didn't agree: his threshold speed was greater than 50 kph, while his race pace barely reached 49 kph. Perhaps, contrary to what we had predicted and observed until then, lactic acid could accumulate at speeds below the threshold. In an attempt to answer this question, we took a blood sample from Francesco immediately after he finished the Firenze-Pistoia time trial.

During the final 2-3 km of the race, Moser slightly surpassed 50 kph and therefore reached his threshold speed. So the lactic acid present in his blood after the race was slightly higher than normal, in keeping with our test. Why then was he incapable of sustaining the pace our tests predicted? After the race we found particularly high levels of another waste product, ammonia—something we had never studied. I don't want to go into complicated details, but it was reasonable to assume, from those tests and from later data, that Moser's diminishing speeds and his inability to pedal at race pace were related to the production and accumulation of this other toxic waste product.

Today we know that there are two thresholds, one that corresponds to lactic acid production and accumulation, the other to ammonia. The build-up of these two waste products doesn't always occur at the same speed. In Moser's case, the ammonia threshold was evidently lower than that of lactic acid. We suspect that this "out of phase" condition occurs primarily in athletes who train for great endurance. Their bodies learn to withstand prolonged efforts by using not only fats and sugars, but also amino acids and proteins, whose utilization results in ammonia production. The fact that the road rider's long workouts don't work well for the middle-distance racer (and vice versa) had been known for a long time. But here we had a biochemical explanation for that fact, one that was never suspected before.

We had found at least a partial explanation both for the results obtained in Mexico and Milan, when Moser stopped training on the road to do specific training for the hour record, and for those in Moscow and Vienna, when Moser continued road racing and long training sessions until the end.

Can Francesco still do it?

After the failures of September and October 1987 and the illuminating results of the time trial, I was asked by journalist Gino Sala to comment on my experiences with Moser and on the setbacks we had just encountered. These were my thoughts:

"More than four years have passed since I began working with Francesco Moser. Together we have done hundreds of tests, traveled thousands of kilometers around the world, measuring his reactions in training, in actual races, and in simulated races. Last Saturday at the time trial from Firenze to Pistoia, I followed Moser during his last road race. Once more he patiently submitted to our sampling and to testing before, during, and after the race.

"Man is not a machine; his behavior is unpredictable and full of unknowns. For every little problem that we resolve, we discover another 10 that we never even suspected. One of the most engrossing unanswered questions concerns the biological decline we inevitably undergo with age. We don't know exactly how and when it manifests itself. Neither do we know just when we begin to go downhill, when the improvements caused by physical maturation or training are overcome by the inevitable decay of advancing age. Maybe, in spite of our efforts, we have seen the first signs of aging in Francesco in the past year. We haven't seen a decline in strength but rather a diminishing capacity to dispose of the waste products produced during very intense physical activity. All the recently collected data, from Moscow to Vienna to Firenze-Pistoia, point to this problem.

"Is it truly a problem of age or simply an off-year? I'm sure this question is very much on Francesco Moser's mind these days. Bad seasons aren't unusual; in fact, they afflict the careers of most athletes. If it's a transitory condition, an off-season caused perhaps by improper training, Moser could decide to make another attempt at the indoor hour record at the end of the six-day season.

"At the Firenze-Pistoia race, I saw a clever sign in the hands of a worried fan. It read: 'Moser, enough already!' I don't know what Moser will decide. In any case, we cannot deny this great athlete and his competitive spirit the desire for a rematch (even against himself) or for success, despite the passing years. Nor can we deny him the opportunity to know and to understand himself completely."

By the end of 1987 almost everyone was convinced that Francesco Moser had irreversibly ended his athletic career and that the two of us had enough good sense to accept the facts and not make the mistake of trying again. Instead, we both were thinking, for different reasons, that the last chapter of the story of the hour record had yet to be written.

The impossible challenge

The last attempt at the hour record seemed, to both Moser and me, an almost impossible challenge. There were many obstacles. Moser was almost 37 years old. He had failed twice before. He had quit road racing, which many observers thought to be important preparation for the hour record.

The public's lack of interest was almost unbearable, but the continual negative comments were even worse. Some of these were good-natured, but others rather cruel: "He's worn out . . . he's got bronchitis . . . he can't do it any longer . . . he'd be better off staying home . . . who do they think they're fooling? . . . he'll eat his words . . . he's doing it for the money . . . not even he believes he can do it . . . it's a sad, undignified decline."

Taken as a whole, these facts, conditions, and comments would have been enough to discourage anyone. We took them as a challenge.

"I want to show what I can do," was the unspoken motivation that pushed Francesco Moser towards his final, incredible record.

Moser's desires for another chance at the record, to make up for his failures and to reach his own personal limits, were valid incentives for anyone and for any objective. But I think he had another motivation, more unusual in an athlete: the desire to understand the reasons behind those failures. Moser's challenge was above all with himself.

Few people around and a bit of quiet at last—that was the unusual atmosphere that surrounded Moser when we met in early February 1988. I was about to leave for the Winter Olympic Games in Calgary, Canada. I expected to be gone for almost a month and, before leaving, I wanted to discuss with Francesco the general program for this final indoor record attempt, if, indeed, we were really going to do it.

Personally, I continued to believe that it was worthwhile to try again. First of all, I felt, as I've already said, that together we had the right, perhaps the duty, to try, even with the risk of failing. Secondly, experience told me that biological processes (including aging, to which many attributed the failures of 1987) show themselves gradually, from one year to the next, and not all at once. It's contrary to the natural order of things that an athlete who is extremely strong at the end of 1986 could decline so significantly in the course of one year. Furthermore, I was gradually becoming convinced that the results recorded at the end of 1987 in Moscow and Vienna were due to training errors (that I felt I had identified) rather than to a rapid decline in Francesco's abilities. I believed all this, but more importantly Moser believed it too. He knew he was worth more than he had shown in the fall of 1987.

Thus, amidst general skepticism, we decided to try again. If we failed, we would have to eat our words. (Someone unkindly reminded me of this on May 21, the day of the record attempt.)

"But what if I do it?" Francesco said to me with the determination of someone bent on revenge.

At Francesco's house we decided on the training program and preparation more in general terms than in day-to-day details. We would follow these guidelines:

—*No more long training sessions.* As with the other record attempts, the major objective of Moser's training was to improve his anaerobic threshold, and thus the speed he could maintain during prolonged effort. In contrast to the previous year, we decided to work more on his strength than on endurance. The available information indicated that endurance training, which is certainly necessary for road racing, could actually be counterproductive in a race that lasts only one hour. We decided to eliminate training sessions of more than three hours.

—*Hard training at altitude.* Another important decision had to do with the training site. We decided that, after a month's work at sea level, Moser should train at altitude a long time. Francesco had already experimented with altitude training on other occasions, but, in my opinion, without the necessary continuity and not for long enough to get appreciable results.

—*A 30-minute trial at race pace before the next attempt.* We didn't even mention the many anaerobic threshold tests we would do during the 90 days of training. Both of us took them for granted. From the start, the only testing we discussed concerned Moser's capacity to maintain race pace without the decrease in speed that afflicted him during the 1987 attempts. We planned two private tests of 30 minutes each, one to be conducted before his altitude training, the other a few days before the record attempt. We decided, for two reasons, to do these at the Stuttgart velodrome: it was to be the site of Moser's final record attempt and we already had data collected on that track from the 30-minute trial two weeks before the Moscow attempt. This would allow for an extremely important comparison. It would show whether, after specific training for the hour record and after a month at altitude, the Moser of 1988 would be himself again, the Moser capable of maintaining a blistering pace without ever slowing down.

—*Experiments with Brandazzi's wheel.* Also on the program was perfecting the equipment, including experiments with the huge rear wheel of Antonio Brandazzi, a technician who worked at Moser's factory.

And so, after Mexico, Milan, Moscow, and Vienna, we started preparing all over again.

Testing

During the winter of 1987-88, Francesco never stopped riding. He participated in some six-day races and trained regularly. So when he began his serious training, he certainly didn't start from zero. He did a series of tests in Sardinia, with the rest of his Chateau d'Ax team, and his results were still among the best. On March 25 at Ferrara, Francesco underwent a series of tests at the track and in the laboratory. These were important: on the basis of the results, we would decide whether or not to continue our program for the final hour record attempt.

Unfortunately, the results were modest. Moser's anaerobic threshold speed, both on the track and on the rollers, was not very high. In addition, his maximal oxygen consumption (VO_2 max—an important measure of an athlete's power during a prolonged effort) was relatively low: 5.2 liters per minute. Michele Ferrari strongly advised Francesco not to continue his preparations for the attempt.

I didn't share Ferrari's opinion. Before setting his hour record in Mexico, Merckx's VO_2 max was half a liter more. While this certainly wasn't a small difference—it's equal to about 1.5 kph—neither was it an impossible gap, given the time we had ahead of us and the altitude training we proposed.

There were two other considerations that kept me from being pessimistic. When Francesco wore the breathing mask to measure his VO_2 max, he performed noticeably worse than under normal conditions. Measured in the laboratory without the mask, his anaerobic threshold was decidedly higher. This difference may have been due to the bronchial asthma that had bothered him occasionally for the previous two years, but it was also a more general finding. We knew that when an athlete performs while wearing a breathing mask, he may easily suffer some loss of power. Also, not all athletes feel the effects equally and Moser suffered more than others.

My other reason for remaining optimistic was this: I believed that, with respect to his available power, Moser could perform particularly well because of his perfect position on the bike. He was extremely aerodynamic.

Neither the laboratory data nor those obtained at the Ferrara velodrome were at all exceptional. However, the cement track at Ferrara is anything but fast. Thus, before making any further decisions, we went to Stuttgart to see how things would go for real.

We planned the usual tests and the first of the two 30-minute trials at race pace that we had promised ourselves. The results on April 8 proved us right (Moser had been optimistic too). As expected, the anaerobic threshold measured on the track in West Germany was definitely higher than it was in Ferrara. Most importantly, Francesco went 48.8 kph in the half-hour trial, just as he had in the test two weeks before the first indoor attempt in Moscow. The difference was that this time we had much more time to prepare and, above all, we were going to use that time to the best advantage with altitude training.

The wheel

Meanwhile, the huge wheel made its appearance. On first impression, I found it ugly. Also, initial comparisons with standard-sized disk wheels showed no appreciable differences. Was the use of the wheel a publicity stunt? No, there were precise theoretical reasons to recommend a wheel with bigger than normal diameter (101 cm). Surface friction would be less; there would be a certain flywheel effect; and finally, once in motion, this wheel couldn't go off course without great difficulty (the so-called gyroscopic effect). In fact, with this wheel Francesco found the bike easier to steer and to keep on course.

During our brief stay in Stuttgart, in addition to getting used to looking at Brandazzi's big wheel, we collected data that showed that it offered a small but consistent advantage. And so we decided to continue preparations for the indoor record attempt and also to adopt the big wheel both in training and in the attempt itself.

This last decision meant a lot of additional work for Moser's framebuilding workshop. After studying the wheel, they would have to construct frames of the right dimensions and proportions. Then Francesco would have to test the new bikes to find out if they performed well—an undertaking not very different from that of a Formula One race car driver.

Training in Bogota

In the previous few years, altitude training had been used increasingly, especially in aerobic sports. We had worked with Francesco at altitude three times and in three different locations (St. Moritz, Passo Fedaia, and Colorado Springs). In my opinion, the results were not very satisfying, even taking into account that those periods at altitude were not long enough and lacked continuity.

But this time we took altitude training more seriously. First of all, there were no other obligations that would interrupt the program. Moreover, the altitude of Bogota, Colombia, (2,700 meters at the track, over 3,000 meters on the road) was higher than the other altitude training. It was high enough to cause severe oxygen deprivation and, therefore, to develop Moser's aerobic system.

From April 14 to May 6, Francesco trained hard at Bogota, first by himself and then with Michele Ferrari, who joined him after a week. As we had agreed, he concentrated more on speed than on endurance. The longest training sessions lasted no more than three hours.

Unfortunately, we couldn't check Francesco's condition in absolute terms. Although training in Bogota had the advantage of altitude, the track was made of cement and was slightly broken up, so it was slow. Therefore we weren't able to compare the new data with what we got before the start in Stuttgart or with data from Mexico City four years earlier. The information we collected did permit us, however, to guide Moser's training and to verify good adaptation to altitude and rapid improvement. Francesco's subjective perceptions of his condition were very good. During a brief trip to Cali, Colombia, at 1,000 meters, his anaerobic threshold and race pace were reassuring, surpassing 50 kph.

On the whole the results, communicated to me by telephone, were promising. Even Michele, who in recent months had been very skeptical about Moser's chances, admitted to a certain optimism when he saw Francesco going so well.

I saw Francesco again after he had trained in Bogota for a month. He was in excellent physical condition, such as I had rarely seen him. Above all, he was determined and confident.

After the altitude training

After training at altitude, an athlete can't suddenly "take off" at sea level. On the contrary, as considerable experience has taught us, he may actually go slower for the first few days. Adapted to an oxygen shortage, the muscles must readapt to a normal oxygen availability. As many as 20 days may be necessary for the benefits of altitude training to become fully evident, and these benefits are brought about not by rest, but by training at progressively greater intensities. Specific training on the track, ideally the same one as for the record attempt, is indispensable during this period.

Unfortunately, the sports center at Stuttgart was used for other sports and concerts and was available for only a few days. We were forced to do some of the training and tests on the tracks at Milan, Bassano del Grappa, and Monaco di Baviera. However, this continuous coming and going didn't make Francesco lose his concentration. The test data improved progressively.

The record for 10 km

We flew to Stuttgart on May 12. The inclement weather in Italy hadn't allowed us to work outdoors, but in Germany we found beautiful spring weather. Ten days had passed since Francesco's return from altitude; it was time to conduct some tests. Moser had intended for some time to make an attempt at the 10 km record. This was too short a test to be truly indicative of his chances at the hour record and his ability to keep up his speed for the distance (the problem in Moscow and Vienna). For that we planned a half-hour trial at race pace a few days later. But the 10-km attempt was an interesting test of ability. What's more, a positive outcome would restore everyone's morale.

On the day before the 10-km attempt, we conducted a test that left me very excited and enthusiastic: Moser easily covered 5 km (with a flying start) at more than 50 kph.

The 10-km record attempt was open to only a few people other than the timekeepers and officials. The standing start was decidedly poor. We hadn't experimented much with that part of the race. Under Moser's powerful stroke, the frame deflected, touching the big rear wheel. Francesco was forced to continue his acceleration in the saddle, which was much less effective than standing on the pedals, and he lost precious time.

To make up this initial disadvantage with respect to Ekimov (the 10-km record holder), Francesco then made the mistake of sprinting the next two laps at more than 54 kph, using anaerobic mechanisms that he hadn't worked on during his altitude training. He immediately closed the gap on Ekimov and even gained a one-second advantage. But inevitably, he began to pay for those overly fast laps. His speed dropped progressively to 49.8 kph. The Soviet was winning again. The event that was supposed to raise everyone's morale risked having the opposite effect. It took all of Moser's physical and mental strength during two final, agonizing laps to even up the result, which seemed already compromised. At the end of an extremely emotion-filled race, the record was his by a second. His time was 11:50.36, and the average speed was 50.650 kph.

Of course, since Ekimov set his 10-km record during his hour record attempt, we presumed that he could have done better than Moser at 10 km. But this was precisely the difference between the two athletes: the Soviet had the speed of a middle-distance cyclist, the Italian the staying power and pace of an endurance athlete. That Moser outdid a middle-distance rider of Ekimov's caliber in a race of this length was, therefore, a very good sign.

This record ride once again showed us the need for a gradual start. A flat-out start makes it impossible to settle quickly into the predetermined race pace, and the rider ends up losing more time than he initially gained. The data proved us to be right. A few days later during the hour record attempt, despite riding the initial laps at a much slower pace, Moser took just slightly longer to reach the 10-km mark, and he did it without any decrease in speed whatsoever.

The test of truth

The indoor 10-km record failed to convince the skeptics; they continued to have little faith in the "old" champion. We, on the other hand, saw evidence of Moser's great physical condition in both the record and our standard anaerobic threshold tests.

We were evicted from Stuttgart for a couple of days by a Sting concert, and each of us decided to spend this time at home. Francesco returned to Stuttgart by way of Monaco. On the outoor track there, in preparation for the 30-minute trial at race pace the next day, he covered 5 km from a flying start in 5:53.96, at an average of 50.853 kph. It was an outstanding performance that showed us, among other things, that he had recovered completely from the hard 10-km ride two days before.

On the evening of May 16, there were no official timekeepers at the Stuttgart velodrome, only a handful of people who were enthusiastic about witnessing the best Moser ever. In the trial from a standing start, which we had long planned as a final test before the record attempt, Francesco covered 25.428 km (89 laps) in 30:27.7. The average speed after the start was 50.24 kph. His pedal action was smooth and easy, and his cardiovascular effort was below the limit we knew he could maintain for an hour. In short, we had wanted to carry out a submaximal test, given that the countdown to the record attempt was only five days, and we found ourselves with a race pace clearly faster than 50 kph.

4
The Stuttgart record
May 21, 1988

Francesco's great performance in the half-hour trial both excited and frightened us. "What if we missed the ideal day?" we asked ourselves. We consoled ourselves with the thought that, barring accident or injury, Moser's physical condition couldn't deteriorate from one day to the next. And this last test could actually serve to refine it.

When we compared this half-hour trial with those on the same track before Moscow and before the trip to Bogota, we had no doubts as to Francesco's excellent physical condition. (See Figure 8.) It's interesting to see a comparison of the three trials: numbers speak louder than words.

Date	Start	Distance	Time	Average speed
9/26/87	flying	24.571 km	30:15.1	48.73
4/8/88	flying	24.571km	30:12.8	48.79
5/16/88	standing	25.428km	30:27.7	50.24*

* excludes the initial lap, covered in 26.39 seconds

The five remaining days didn't pass easily. We had to resist the temptation to run further tests just to reassure ourselves that all was going well. Moser's single objective was to get back that indispensable freshness by training just enough to maintain his condition. In contrast, we worked hard on the technical aspects.

First of all, we discussed which gear to use on the basis of Moser's power (which in this case was at least 50.200 kph) and the cadence to be maintained during the record attempt. Francesco felt comfortable pedaling at 102 rpm, a cadence slightly lower than those of the previous attempts. Thus, we aimed for a roll-out of 8.21 meters per pedal stroke. This was obtained with a 47/18 gear, which, at 50.200 kph, required at least 102 rpm.

We also discussed at length what pace Moser should maintain. My greatest fears were a too-fast start and variations in speed. To prevent these problems, we decided to signal Moser the elapsed time for every lap during the record attempt. We even established the lap times Francesco had to stay within: a maximum of 20.57 seconds (equivalent to 50 kph) and a minimum of 20.37 seconds (50.494 kph). He was absolutely prohibited from going below 20 seconds per lap (51.428 kph). At that speed the excessive lactic acid build-up would seriously compromise his pace.

The atmosphere was calm. I felt among us the confidence that had been lacking for months. Some Italian emigrants, many of them from Moser's home province of Trent, served as interpreters and helped us organize the attempt. One person even took some vacation time from work to help us full time. We often dined in a small restaurant owned by people from Trent, headquarters of a club of "Trentini." They smoked too much and I complained about it, but we felt at home and ate well. We slept in a small hotel near the track, as secluded as necessary.

Thursday, May 19, three days after the 30-minute trial and two days before the record attempt, we could resist no longer and allowed ourselves a last, brief check to "test the legs." Francesco pedaled "normally" at 48.9 kph for 5 km and then in the next 5 km went directly to a race pace of 50.96 kph. He did this easily and without the obvious fatigue suffered in similar tests before the Moscow attempt. Finally, we were ready for the rematch.

Final thoughts

Also on this occasion many people came from far away —perhaps more to show solidarity and to hail a champion on his retirement than to witness an hour record. The fact that the newspapers hadn't given the attempt much coverage meant that the fans' interest wasn't created by publicity. But Francesco had also gotten us into a bad habit: we no longer realized what it meant to cover 50 km in one hour on a bicycle. Yet no one other than Moser had done it. And only two athletes had surpassed 49 km at sea level: Moser himself (49.802 km) and Ekimov (49.672 km).

With Michele Ferrari and Ilario Casoni, I repeatedly examined the test data from the two weeks since Moser's return from Bogota. On the basis of this data, we were convinced that our training program (primarily for strength, little for endurance, and more training at altitude) had enabled Francesco to attain an unprecedented physical condition. We believed that the indoor hour record held by Ekimov (not underestimated as in Moscow but confronted with the utmost seriousness) could not escape Moser this time. And so began the fifth record attempt on May 21, 1988.

By now it had become a ritual: Moser warmed up for 45 minutes behind a motorcycle and then we conducted a test. He put on the aerodynamic clothing, rode another few laps, and then the race started—all of this with one eye on the clock and with emotions in check. The results of the pre-race test certainly weren't among the best in the past few days. Even Francesco felt the impending race, the crowd, the television cameras. We saw it in the data, which showed production of a lot of stress hormones, adrenaline in particular. The same thing had happened in Moscow, though much more strikingly.

This is not to say that an excess of adrenaline changes things radically. The outcome in Moscow certainly cannot be explained by excessive tension alone. However, the emotions can play dirty tricks. For example, they can make an athlete consume precious glycogen reserves before the start, reserves that will be needed later in the race. Or else they can induce a breathless start, even too fast a start, with the resulting penalty of lactate build-up.

Those thoughts crossed my mind while the computer, quick and impersonal, traced the graph of a just-performed and not very exciting test. We held a quick consultation——Francesco, Michele, and I. Though the start was imminent, we decided to do a series of laps at increasing speeds and then a few more at about 50 kph. We wanted to let Moser's body discharge the excessive pre-race tension and reduce his stress. During this additional test the data collected by the heart rate monitor gradually improved. It would have been worthwhile to continue a little longer, but the international television broadcast was at hand, and we had to go to the starting line.

I knew from experience that as long as you're training, all goes well. But then, when it's time to race and you want total concentration, you're disturbed by every little thing that's out of the ordinary. So I never expected that Francesco, at the start of perhaps the most important race of his life, would willingly accept my suggestion to monitor and record his heart rate during the hour record attempt. He did agree and thus the race also became a final verification of the research we had conducted together since 1983. In the photographs taken before the start, Moser is seen pressing a button on his heart rate monitor to start the precious recording, one we would later study with great care. During the record attempt, the continuous heart rate display gave him valuable additional information about his work intensity and his operating reserves.

The timekeeper and his colleagues, who had come from Milan specifically for this event, provided us with a small monitor on which we could see the elapsed time and average speed of each lap, and the cumulative average speed. We placed it alongside the track, half a lap away from the timekeeper, so we would have time to signal the data to Francesco only slightly out of phase. We wanted

Moser to know his times as he rode for two reasons: to help him avoid starting out too fast, and to reduce to a minimum the inevitable and counterproductive fluctuations in speed throughout the hour.

As it turned out, partly because of our screaming "Slow!" at the start and partly because an hour can be a very long time and he instinctively saved himself a bit, Moser rode constantly at a submaximal level. We saw it in several ways. On receiving our signal of a slow lap, he could make up the difference immediately in the next lap. In addition, his final crescendo was only possible for an athlete in perfect physical condition with complete mental clarity. And finally, his heart rate was certainly below maximal.

His heart rate pattern was very interesting. On the average, it turned out to be only one beat above his anaerobic threshold heart rate, with variations that corresponded to his variations in speed—a very important fact physiologically. Only in the end, coinciding with his hardest effort (the last lap was ridden at more than 54 kph, faster than in Mexico) did his heart rate reach its maximum.

I remember very little about the race, involved as I was in signaling times and average speeds and making sure that everything went right. In one hour at sea level, Moser rode 50.644 km, or 1,213 meters further than Merckx's hour record at altitude, a distance that had seemed almost unbeatable four years earlier.

After the final record

I also remember only fragments of the period after the race. Many people were emotional. A journalist who had chronicled cycling during the "heroic era" cried. He had the sensation of having witnessed the last act of a great champion and perhaps even of a certain kind of cycling. With Francesco, he concluded a chapter of his own life too.

I remember Moser's slightly bitter outburst against those who had doubted and criticized him, especially on the occasion of his final hour record. His reaction showed how much, and for how long a time, he had been upset by the resentful criticism of some people and the coldness of others.

I also remember the drug-control tests, conducted outside Italy at our request by West German personnel, who both collected and analyzed the urine samples. The samples were again sent to Cologne to the best-equipped and most rigorous drug control laboratory in the world. (Its director, Manfred Donike, was in charge of technical aspects and personnel for drug testing at the 1988 Olympics in Seoul, South Korea.) The unequivocal response was that in Stuttgart, as in Mexico, Milan, Moscow, and Vienna, drugs had nothing to do with this extraordinary athlete's performance.

A helicopter carried us away. Gazing down as the Hans Martin Schleyer Velodrome grew rapidly smaller, I realized with a mixture of joy and regret that the adventure was over. Finally stretched out and relaxed, we talked as we flew towards Frankfurt, our destination for that evening. We thought about Ekimov.

"I don't think he'll try again," Francesco told me.

I agreed. The gap between the two records seemed, indeed, unbridgeable.

Comparing Moser and Merckx

Francesco continued to astonish me. Two days after the Stuttgart record, I proposed one last day of testing, so we could compare the data obtained two and a half months earlier with the current data. He came and spent the night in Ferrara and, although he loves to sleep late, was ready to go to work first thing in the morning. We warmed up together on the road and then went to the track for the first series of tests. Later we went to the laboratory to measure his VO_2 max.

I have never approved of VO_2 max tests, mostly because they're impractical. The necessary equipment is too cumbersome to be used in the field; the breathing mask makes the athlete uncomfortable and can even generate a sense of

claustrophobia, with consequent nonphysiological breathing difficulties. That's why, in my 20 years of sports
research, I've always preferred field tests.

Then why perform these tests now, when the record
attempts were over? I wanted to compare Moser's data
with those of other athletes, Merckx in particular, who was
tested for VO_2 max in two different laboratories before his
Mexico City hour record. The VO_2 max value seemed to be
the only possible means of comparing these two great
athletes directly, given that there had been too many
technological and other changes in cycling to allow for a
direct comparison. The difference between Merckx's and
Moser's records could be attributed to the bicycle, the
wheels, the track surface, and the different clothing. Moser
might even have been less physically strong than Merckx
but beat him anyway, thanks to the mechanical and other
technical advances that took place between 1972 and 1988.

After carefully calibrating the equipment, we did the test.
Francesco pedaled as if he intended to race for another 10
years. The values obtained were considerably better, of
course, than those in March before his altitude training. His
threshold speeds (measured in the laboratory and on the
track) were 18 percent higher than those of March 26. His
VO_2 max similarly improved (19.2 percent), having increased from 5.20 to 6.20 liters per minute.

And Merckx? His VO_2 max values, measured in two
different laboratories, were 5.55 and 5.70 lpm. Therefore,
Moser's "engine" consumed at least a half liter more
oxygen and was 8.7 percent more powerful than the
Belgian's. Given that for the hour record a rider uses
aerobic power almost exclusively (except at the start and
finish), one can safely say that the 1988 Moser, placed on
the track under the same conditions and on the same bike
as Merckx in 1972, would have ridden approximately 50.8
km in one hour. (This calculation takes into account that
the work performed in cycling increases with speed cubed.
Merckx's distance, 49.431, cubed is 120780.8799. Adding
8.7 percent for Moser's greater VO_2 max yields 131288.8165.

The cube root of that total is 50.824, the theoretical distance Moser would have ridden.)

Today we know, and it must be said in fairness, that Merckx was not at his peak form in Mexico. First of all, he had just finished a season of road racing, a situation we now know to be counterproductive as preparation for the hour record. Moreover, he wasn't acclimatized to altitude; rather, he had been at altitude for only a few days. So he presumably made the record ride at the worst possible moment, that of the crisis point in acclimatization. (I have always thought that this fact was partly responsible for his terrible state after the race.) Finally, Merckx hadn't carried out the specific training that's possible today, much less trained for a month at 3,000 meters in Bogota.

Eddy Merckx was an extraordinary athlete. His hour record, which for years discouraged others from even making an attempt, frightened us as well, but it also served as an objective and an incentive. Without his 49.431 km to surpass, perhaps things would have gone much differently for us. The Belgian champion's record must not be under-estimated even today. Let's not forget that only two men, Moser and Ekimov, have succeeded in breaking it since it was set in 1972.

This said, the difference between the Moser of 1988 and the Merckx of 1972 remains, and it is considerable.

Many people asked and even argued about what the indoor hour record could possibly add to Moser's other hour records, especially after the two failed attempts in Moscow and Vienna. For years it was almost obligatory to attempt the hour record on the magical Vigorelli velodrome in Milan. That way it was fair; it offered a means of comparing a cyclist with the champions of the past—with Coppi, Anquetil, Baldini, etc. Then Merckx, following Ole Ritter's example, sought out the more favorable conditions of high altitude to establish his great hour record. And he succeeded, obtaining a result that discouraged every possible contender for years. From that time on, the sacred site of the hour record became Mexico City.

Today we know that an altitude record, transferred to sea level, is worth about two kilometers less. Taking this into account, we find that Merckx's record was not as great as that of Ferdinand Bracke (48.093 km), set on the Olympic Velodrome in Rome on October 10, 1967.

For technical and scientific reasons I always considered the indoor record the most significant goal for Moser, above all for its reproducibility. If we examine things closely, we see that the altitude records are anything but codifiable. In fact, air resistance and oxygen availability vary considerably at 600, 2,000, and 3,000 meters.

Then how can we establish standard conditions in which to take measurements? In the outdoor records, the athlete's performance is strongly influenced by wind, temperature, and humidity. So the success of a record attempt can sometimes depend on luck, on finding a day when the atmospheric conditions are favorable and the athlete is at his physical peak.

In short, if I were an athlete wanting to attempt the hour record I would do it on an indoor velodrome, sheltered from changing atmospheric conditions, and at sea level, less than 600 meters. I would go up against the "real" hour record and the hardest one to break: Moser's 50.644 km set in Stuttgart.

Closing notes

During the years of research, Francesco Moser demonstrated patience but above all curiosity. He wanted to know and understand. It was thanks to his curiosity that we all learned things we never knew before, some of them having to do with sports, others more generally with how the human machine functions.

Biology is a science of individuals. Just as medicine doesn't exist without the individual patient, physiology is best served by the study of a single human being; later we can apply our findings to human beings in general. The story of Moser the athlete is the story of how the human machine works. In order to sustain its vital functions, this machine requires the continuous combustion of sugars and fats with oxygen, which is breathed in and transported to the cells by the cardiovascular system. It's the story of the mechanism that enables us to do sustained work, of the engine that drives not only the muscles, but also the entire organism, the heart, the brain.... Good health depends on its efficiency.

Over the years we have learned to measure and improve the power of this engine. We have seen that its efficient functioning is important not only to the athlete but also to the common man, who often suffers the effects of inactivity and overindulgence. To continue the analogy, training Francesco Moser was like working on a Formula One racing car, the fine tuning of which eventually leads to improvements in the family car.

There's nothing like doing something for many years to make you learn how to do it correctly and to understand its significance completely. Moser submitted to hundreds of our tests, which, with his help, came to be a reliable means of evaluating cyclists. To continue the analogy, the heart rate monitor became an instrument that can be used like the tachometer in a car. The speed of the athlete or the car depends on the gear, the terrain, the atmospheric conditions, and the type of fuel the engine is burning. The heart rate monitor, on the basis of the athlete's ability (determined in preliminary tests), measures the effort and the power reserves independently of the many other variables that come into play. The many tests we did contributed to Francesco Moser's maturation as an athlete who is fully aware of his own abilities.

The hour record athlete

Based on my experiences with Francesco, I offer the following guidelines on the type of athlete and training program suitable for the hour record.

—A road rider is what's needed. A track rider who wanted to challenge himself with the hour record would have to give up his sprint and commit himself to a kind of training that would change this characteristic into pacing—something that's not always possible and that takes a long time, sometimes years.

—A tall road rider who has a great aerobic capacity (high anaerobic threshold, high VO_2 max) and good aerodynamic qualities is the most likely candidate. In other words, the ideal hour record rider would be a road racer particularly suited to long time trials on flat courses.

—This cyclist should stop road racing for a while and devote himself for several months to improving his anaerobic threshold by training at altitude and on the track. As the date of the record attempt approaches, he must test his physical condition by doing some tests at race pace on the same track as the planned attempt.

—Finally, he must be very stable psychologically, able to withstand the long preparation periods and the stress of public attention in order to go to the starting line calm and focused.

How much did Moser pay for his hour records in terms of physical well-being? Especially after the failed indoor record attempts of 1987, there were those who said, "Look at how he's aged. These repeated attempts at the hour record must have been hard on him."

The truth is, at 37 years of age it's normal for a few gray hairs to appear. Then, with hard training, the body loses some of its fat deposits, and the skin is less taut and appears more wrinkled. (Rarely was Francesco leaner than in Stuttgart, when his weight dropped to 74.5 kg. He would have climbed very well indeed.) Being so thin, Moser may have looked like a man marked by fatigue.

But that wasn't the case. Francesco got his best results in Stuttgart and reached his maximal physical efficiency, probably not only for the 1983-88 period but for his entire career. That is, he attained his full athletic maturity, which is quite different from premature aging!

Because of continuous fluctuations in lactic acid it's much

more tiring to race on the road than it is to train and race at a constant pace. In the latter case, one doesn't exceed the anaerobic threshold, and thus there's no lactic acid build-up.

This is probably why some middle-distance riders such as Oersted, Ekimov, and perhaps even Merckx paid for the hour record more than Moser did. These athletes were superior to Moser in a race that lasts a few minutes (for example, the 5,000-meter pursuit), where the anaerobic lactic acid mechanisms they are particularly endowed with came into play. But when the effort lasted longer, the situation was reversed: Moser could continue without changing pace, while the middle-distance racers were forced to slow down, penalized by their active anaerobic mechanisms which led to lactic acid build-up over time. These decreases in speed are evident in Oersted, Ekimov, and even Merckx (see Fig. 10), all of whom were decidedly put to the test towards the end of the hour. Moser, on the other hand, with a less powerful anaerobic mechanism, didn't run the risk of accumulating too much lactic acid. In addition, with his specific experience in the hour record, he knew how to avoid acid-producing efforts. In fact, Francesco always finished his record rides, even the failed ones, in an enviably fresh condition, often accelerating at the end.

If I had to identify the predominant feeling during my five years of work with Moser, I would say it was uncertainty. Contrary to what might appear to an outsider, nothing was mathematical; everything was debatable. Not once, before the various tests, were we sure about the outcome because, in every one of the seven attempts, we introduced significant changes in equipment and training. Moreover, even when you repeat a training program exactly, you can never be sure of obtaining the same results in competition because the athlete also unpredictably changes with the passing of time. This uncertainty, though exhausting at the time, is now one of the pleasant memories.

Whom do we thank?

It's difficult to list the many individuals who contributed, in both large and small ways, to Francesco Moser's records. I could mention Carlo Potrich, the man from Trent who was "transplanted" (not without trauma) to Stuttgart, but then I might forget Oberto Cortesi. So, in order to make fewer mistakes, I prefer to remember the groups of supporters who surrounded Moser during these years.

—*The Moser family.* The patriarchal family from Palu di Giovo participated in Francesco's hour records, each member having his own duties. The records were partly theirs. Francesco's brother Enzo probably contributed the most, and very patiently.

—*The fans.* It was a great help to have people around who believed in Moser and supported him on every occasion, including the least happy ones. Francesco attracted the loyalty of many different people, including me. Of this group I mention the leader of the Moser Club, Italo Garbari, to represent the club's 8,000 members and all the rest of us.

—*The journalists.* Over the course of these years, I came to understand the power of this group to influence public opinion, even in sports. The newspapers always gave good coverage to Moser's record attempts, although it's true they were almost obliged to. Not all the journalists I met worked hard enough on checking the facts before making them public. But in many of these journalists I saw enthusiasm, competence, and a love of cycling. I established cordial friendships with some, those who followed our research work closely, knowledgeably, and sympathetically. Of this group, I must mention Sergio Meda, Fulvio Astori, and Giacomo Santini, who did everything in their power to coordinate the efforts of their colleagues in Mexico City, Moscow, Vienna, and Stuttgart.

—*The sponsors.* Although I've always carefully avoided getting involved in their commercial activities, I must acknowledge that, without the sponsors and their willingness to invest in Francesco Moser's possibilities, we wouldn't have been able to do anything. Certainly their support was based partly on their own interests and on Moser's ability to capture public attention, to make news. That in itself was a guarantee of success, regardless of the race results. However, one can't help but also recognize an involvement that often went beyond strictly marketing interests.

I also thank my daughter Maria for having saved me from numerous inconsistencies and grammatical errors in writing this book.

What remains?

When you reach the top of a difficult mountain climb, you're happy to have made it. Above all, this is what remains to us: the satisfaction of having lived through a challenging human and scientific adventure.

Francesco Moser's special magnetism brought out the fans and journalists for every hour record attempt. Three hundred members of his fan club flew from Italy to Mexico City to witness the first record ride.

"If you see it's not going well, make me stop," Moser said before the first sea-level attempt at the Vigorelli Velodrome in Milan. "I knew he suffered greatly in his struggle against the wind," said author Francesco Conconi (above right), "but I let him continue, for how do you stop an athlete who is winning?" The result was a world record of 48.543 kilometers, but Moser had been forced to adopt an unusual riding position, resulting in terrible cramps in both legs (facing page). "I believe that I suffered more than Merckx did," he said.

Only a week after the first sea-level attempt, Moser was ready to try again (facing page). This time the conditions were perfect and he rode to a new record of 49.802 kilometers. Through all the successes and failures, Moser was encouraged and supported by family and friends, including (above) his wife Carla, their two children, and Francesco's brother Enzo.

Altitude record: Olympic Sports Center Velodrome in Mexico City

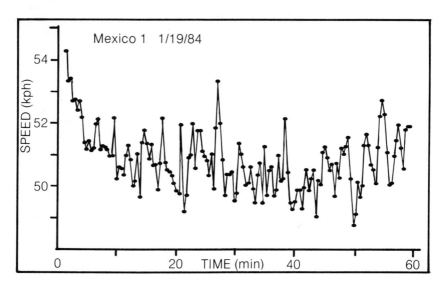

Mexico 1   1/19/84

Speed per lap for the first record (50.802 km)

The graph of Moser's first record, seen in retrospect, indicates a certain inexperience, shown by the large fluctuations in speed during the ride. These variations in pace can be attributed only partially to the wind, which didn't affect the attempt very much. Actually, I think they were due to the fact that Moser was still not used to maintaining a constant pace.

The overly fast start (more than 54 kph on the second and third lap) forced Moser into a recuperation period that lasted until minute 20. Only towards the half-hour mark do we see two faster sections, with peaks as high as 53 kph, indicating that the initial fatigue had diminished. In the second half-hour the speed was more constant. Moser had overcome the initial tension and found his rhythm, finishing in crescendo.

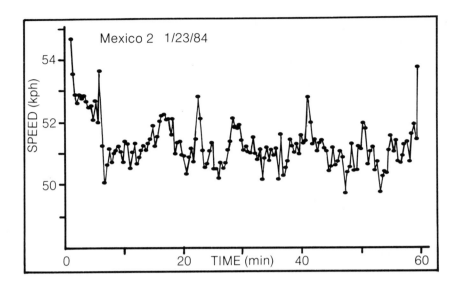

Speed per lap for the second record (51.151 km)

Despite the wind that definitely affected his performance, Moser demonstrated more calmness and mental clarity than in the first attempt (by then the Mexican expedition had succeeded) and maintained a more constant pace. The effort was clearly greater than four days earlier. This was shown by the fact that Francesco sat on the nose of his saddle.

Moser wanted to beat the 5- and 20-km records. Thus the graph shows accelerations at the 6th and 23rd minutes, where there are two intermediate peaks. At the end of this difficult ride Moser still had the energy for a good final crescendo.

Milan: the two records at sea level on an outdoor track

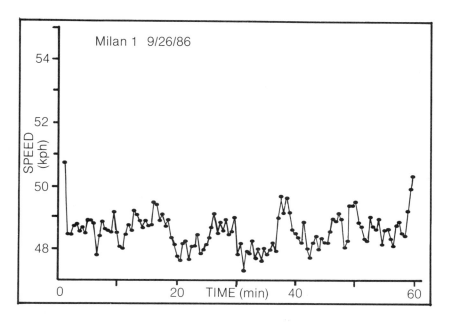

Milan 1 9/26/86

Speed per lap for the third record (48.543 km)

Although the speed was relatively modest, the effort was maximal from the first lap. To keep a constant tempo in the sections against the wind, which gusted to 30 kph, Moser had to give it his all. The lactic acid that's produced in this situation can't be reduced in the few seconds of tailwind each lap. Therefore, it accumulated lap by lap, making the ride almost unbearable.

The wind slackened a little around minute 40 and Moser could recuperate and finish with a small acceleration. He beat Oersted's Bassano record (48.145 km), but the lactic acid build-up, combined with the unusual riding position he had to use because of the wind, brought on extremely painful leg cramps after the finish.

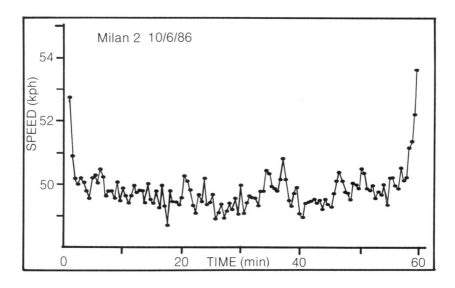

Speed per lap for the fourth record (49.802 km)

Moser was perfect, both in the start, which was decisive but not excessive, and in the distribution of effort, which shows very slight fluctuations, descending only once below 49 kph. At the end Francesco accelerated decisively, showing his excellent condition and large reserve of strength. With a little more conviction and a slightly bigger gear he could have reached 50 km.

The failures of autumn 1987

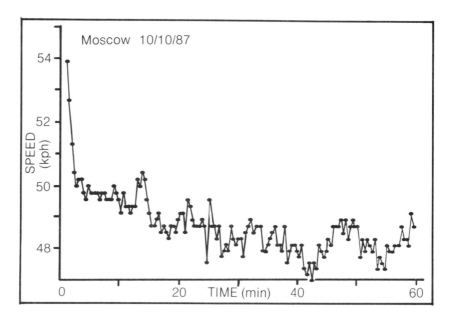

Speed per lap for the Moscow attempt (48.637 km)

Moser started very fast, but after only five laps his speed dropped below 50 kph. He kept up the fight to maintain his pace, but all his efforts were in vain. His speed progressively slowed to 47 kph, at around minute 42. Not even in Milan against the wind had he slowed to that speed.

Despite the discouragement of these negative results, the silence of the fans, and some hissing by the Muscovites, Moser continued proudly and succeeded in increasing his speed a little at the end. But he was far from the planned 50 km. To have broken the indoor professional record was a small consolation—in reality we were still 1 km behind Ekimov.

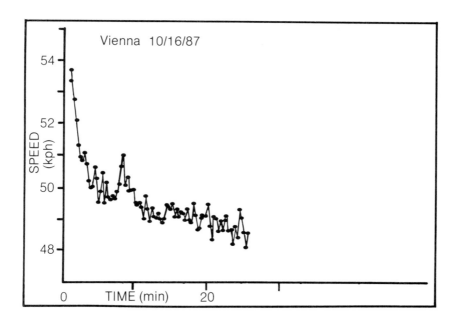

Speed per lap for the Vienna attempt (stopped after 27 minutes)

It was useless, he just couldn't do it. Another very fast start, followed by an inexorable decline. Although Moser was doing better than in Moscow and we could predict a result of 49 km, Ekimov's record was out of reach. The ride was stopped after 27 minutes.

The 10-km indoor record and half-hour tests at Stuttgart

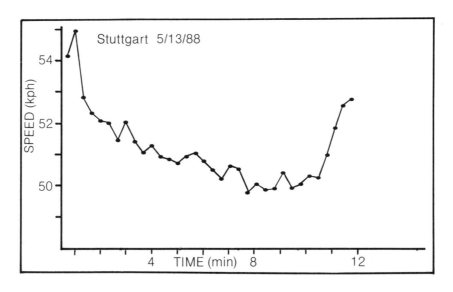

Speed per lap for the 10-km record

We used this record attempt to verify Moser's condition before the hour record. Reviewing the graph, I had one negative observation, and that was about Moser's suicidal distribution of effort. He started out very fast, riding his second lap at 54 kph. From the side of the track, I signaled to him that he was seven seconds 'behind' Ekimov's average record speed. Moser's response was to ride the next lap at almost 55 kph and close the gap on Ekimov. But then Francesco paid for those two fast laps, dropping to less than 50 kph.

With four laps to go, Moser was almost a second behind Ekimov. Spurred on by his own pride, he gave it his all in the last 3 laps and finished the 10 km in 11:50.36, slightly more than a second faster than Ekimov. During the hour record attempt eight days later, by distributing his effort correctly and by expending less energy, Moser passed the 10-km mark at 11:53.79.

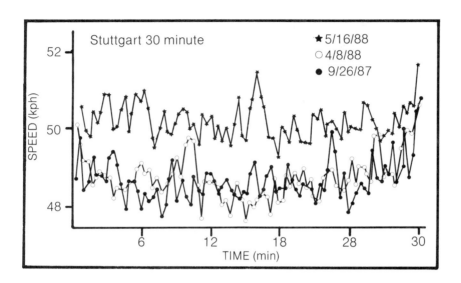

Speed per lap for the three 30-minute trials

The Stuttgart velodrome was easy to reach and usually available, so we used it three times to verify Moser's ability to maintain an adequate race pace during 30-minute trials.

—*First trial* (dots), September 26, 1987, 15 days before the Moscow attempt: From a flying start, Moser rode 24.57 km in 30:15.16 for an average speed of 48.73 kph. His effort was submaximal; in fact, his average heart rate was lower than usual for a race. There were still 15 days before the hour record attempt, and we hoped to close the gap on Ekimov.

—*Second trial* (circles), April 8, 1988, immediately before Moser's departure for Bogota: From a flying start, Moser rode 24.57 km in 30:12.84 for an average speed of 48.79 kph. We were very satisfied with this trial. For one thing, his speed increased from the 15-minute mark on. We still had 43 days before the hour record attempt, and we hadn't yet done the crucial altitude training.

—*Third trial* (stars), May 16, 1988, three days after the 10-km record and five days before the final hour record attempt: We began this trial from a standing start. Moser rode 25.43 km in 30:27.82. Omitting the initial lap, his average speed for 88 laps (the equivalent of a flying start) was 50.24 kph. He rode only two of those laps at a pace slower than Ekimov's average hour record speed. Francesco's high average speed, his easy pedaling, his sub-maximal effort, and his increased speed at the end convinced us that, this time, Francesco would do it.

The Stuttgart record

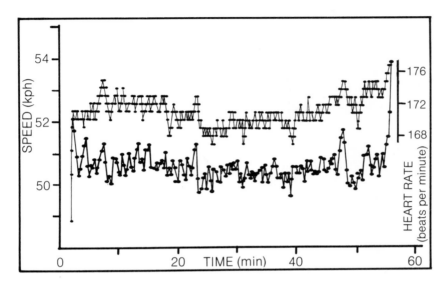

Speed per lap (lower line, scale at left) and heart rate (upper line, scale at right) for the Stuttgart hour record (50.644 km)

This effort might just represent Francesco Moser at his best. He started cautiously, his pace controlled and uniform, and in only one lap did he go slightly below 50 kph. The graph shows an increase to more than 52 kph after 50 minutes, but too much time was left for Francesco to maintain that pace until the end. So he held back a few minutes before his "grand finale." He rode the last lap at more than 54 kph.

The relationship between speed and heart rate is surprising. It shows that, even at 50.600 kph, Moser never accumulated lactic acid. Moreover, he never used his glycogen reserves. These are two signs that his effort was submaximal. His average heart rate for the hour was only one beat higher than his anaerobic threshold rate.

Comparing the records and the riders

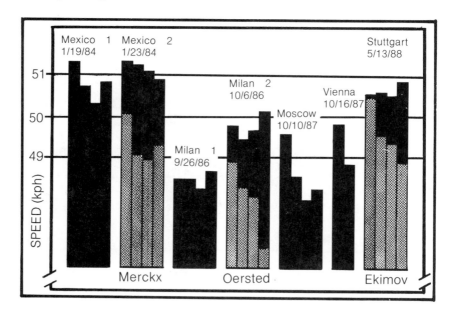

Distribution of Moser's effort in the seven hour record attempts (black columns) and comparisons to Merckx, Oersted, and Ekimov (gray columns)

This figure subdivides the six hour record attempts that we finished, as well as the terminated Vienna attempt, into 15-minute fractions. Each attempt is thus divided into four columns (only two for Vienna) to illustrate the speed maintained in the first, second, third, and fourth successive quarters of each race. With this graph, we can see Moser's distribution of effort and staying power during the various attempts.

In three of the seven attempts (Mexico 2, Moscow, and Vienna), his race pace dropped off. In Mexico, the drop was caused by the wind, which forced Francesco to ride in spurts, not uniformly, and which gradually reduced his power. The indoor attempts in Moscow and Vienna show the problem Moser was having in late 1987—he was unable to maintain a constant fast pace over time. In both of these attempts, his speed dropped continuously and progressively in spite of his great effort, except for the final laps in Moscow.

The record with a uniform distribution of effort (Milan 1) represents another swindle by the wind, which was strong during the first part (this cost Moser a lot) and a little less so in the second part. Thus, he was able to maintain his speed in the second part despite the tremendous effort he expended in the first.

Two attempts (Milan 2 and Stuttgart) show increasing speed. On those occasions Moser had power reserves that surpassed both his and our expectations. At Milan 2, in particular, we found ourselves with an athlete who was capable of riding 50 km but who was using a gear suitable for little more than 49 kph, the race pace we had anticipated.

In the last half hour of the Stuttgart attempt, Francesco's effort was superhuman. He rode faster than in the first Mexico record. In the last 10 minutes, he even surpassed the speed maintained in the absolute hour record (Mexico 2). And to think that the difference between altitude and sea level is a couple of kilometers!

This graph also compares the distribution of effort and speeds of Moser's records (black columns) with three preceding records (gray columns): at altitude against Eddy Merckx, on an outdoor velodrome at sea level against Hans Henrik Oersted, and indoors against Viatcheslav Ekimov. The three preceding records are far below the new limits set by Moser.

Equipment used in the five hour records

	Record location and date				
	Mexico 1-19-84	**Mexico 1-24-84**	**Milan 9-26-86**	**Milan 10-3-86**	**Stuttgart 5-21-88**
Weight of bicycle	11.0 kg 24.2 lb	11.0 kg 24.2 lb	8.5 kg 18.7 lb	8.5 kg 18.7 lb	12.5 kg 27.5 lb
Front wheel:					
type	lenticular	lenticular	lenticular	lenticular	lenticular
diameter (cm/in)	66/26	66/26	61.5/24.2	61.5/24.2	67.0/26.4
tubulars	105 g	105 g	100 g	100 g	120 g
Rear wheel:					
type	lenticular	lenticular	flat disk	flat disk	lenticular
diameter (cm/in)	71/28	71/28	66.5/26.2	69.0/27.2	101.0/39.8
tubulars	120 g	120 g	100 g	100 g	200 g
Gear used (chainring/ sprocket)	56/15	57/15	57/15	51/14	47/18
Wheel development (meters per pedalstroke)	8.03	8.17	7.91	7.88	8.28
Average cadence (pedalstrokes per minute)	105.4	104.3	102.3	105.3	101.9
Distance covered (km)	50.802	51.151	48.543	49.802	50.644

What is the
Test Conconi?

The test that Dr. Conconi developed and used extensively in guiding Moser's training for the hour records is based on monitoring an athlete's heart rate during exercise and comparing the recorded rates to work output (expressed in speed for a runner, speed cubed for a cyclist due to increased air resistance at higher speeds). The purpose is to determine at what speed/heart rate combination the athlete begins to accumulate lactic acid, a product of anaerobic work, at a faster rate than the blood can carry it away from the working muscles.

This level of effort is critical in endurance sports because it represents the amount of work the athlete is capable of performing for a long time. It is commonly called the anaerobic threshold (AT) because below this level the athlete uses primarily aerobic means of energy production (using oxygen to break down organic fuels), while above this level, anaerobic means of energy production (without oxygen) are employed to the extent that lactic acid begins to accumulate in the muscles. If allowed to continue, this lactic acid buildup interferes with the muscle activities and the athlete is forced to decrease his effort or stop exercising altogether. In order to perform best in an endurance event, an athlete must stay at or just below AT, with only brief excursions into the anaerobic zone. Under varying conditions (or with changes in fitness levels) the speed at AT may change, but the AT heart rate will remain constant or change only slightly.

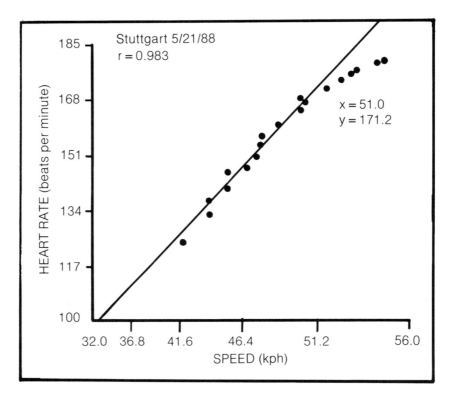

This graph of the Test Conconi performed by Moser before the Stuttgart record shows his anerobic threshold at 51 kph and 171.2 bpm. From 1983 to 1988 Moser performed hundreds of these tests to help determine his training intensity and to test the effects of equipment changes.

The anaerobic threshold is a physiological phenomenon that has been recognized for many years. What Dr. Conconi discovered is that AT can be determined with relative ease by monitoring heart rate. Conconi made this discovery in the late 1970s by observing his own heart rate during a regular training run. Prior to Conconi's finding, AT determination required expensive, inconvenient, and not readily available testing methods such as blood sampling and respiratory gas analysis. Use of a heart rate monitor makes AT testing more practical, economical, and accessible to athletes.

In cycling, the Test Conconi is usually carried out on a velodrome, which makes it easy to measure the distance covered to calculate average speed. Wearing a heart rate monitor, the cyclist warms up and then rides a series of laps, starting at moderate speed and increasing the speed slightly each lap or half-lap. (A cycle speedometer is useful for this purpose.) Meanwhile, a test assistant records the time to calculate average speeds and heart rate for each lap. The heart rates can either be called out to the assistant by the cyclist at the end of each lap or stored in the memory of the heart rate monitor for later recall. The latter method is preferable because several heart rates can be recorded for each lap and then averaged to give a more accurate measure of the cyclist's effort.

The data is then analyzed to determine at what speed/ heart rate combination the cyclist reached AT. It's possible to determine AT through mathematical analysis, but the numbers are often plotted on a graph (heart rate versus speed cubed) for visual verification. The initial part of the test should reveal a linear relationship between speed and heart rate (as speed increases, heart rate goes up). When the athlete reaches AT, the linearity is lost because heart rate, an indicator of aerobic energy production, increases at a slower rate than speed, which continues to increase at the same rate due to help from anaerobic energy production. (On a graph, AT will appear as a point of deflection or 'knee' in the line.)

Once an athlete knows his AT, he can use it to maximize training. In his work with runners, Conconi determined that improvements in aerobic power, the most critical factor in endurance performance, can best be achieved by training at or just below AT heart rate (within 10%). By regularly repeating the Test Conconi, an athlete can determine the effectiveness of his training and whether it needs to be modified.

In his work with Moser, Dr. Conconi also used the Test Conconi to determine the ideal equipment for the hour records (bicycle frame and components, wheels, clothing, etc.). This was accomplished by having Moser ride at his AT heart rate while using various kinds of equipment and observing with which combinations he could attain the highest average speeds.

Since its development, the Test Conconi has been applied, misapplied, and modified by scientists, coaches, and athletes all over the world. So, in addition to carrying out further research and working with an ever-increasing number of athletes in various sports, Dr. Conconi also has responded to numerous requests to present and explain the test and its applications.

In this book, Conconi compares Francesco Moser to a Formula One racing car, the fine tuning of which improves performance. Such fine tuning not only improves the fastest race vehicle, but the family car as well. Thanks to the continuing efforts of Conconi and his colleagues at Italy's University of Ferrara, not only world- and national-class athletes, but those of us with less powerful engines can use this knowledge to improve our performance.

Patricia Ennis

About the author
and the translator

Francesco Conconi, M.D., is a professor of applied bio-chemistry at the University of Ferrara, Italy. During the past 20 years, he has become increasingly involved in sportsmedicine and was instrumental in establishing the university's Center for Research Applied to Sports.

Conconi is best known among cyclists, runners, and other endurance athletes as creator of the Test Conconi, a method of optimizing aerobic training by monitoring heart rates. His most famous research subject is Italian cycling champion Francesco Moser, whom Conconi assisted in all of his world hour record attempts and throughout the final years of his professional cycling career, as related in this book. Conconi has also worked closely with Maria Canins, two-time winner of the Tour de France Feminin (1985-86).

Born in Como, Italy, in 1935, Conconi received a degree in medicine in 1959 and spent two years doing research at Columbia University in New York (1964-65). He began working with runners in the 1970s and in 1982 published the first of a series of scientific journal articles explaining the Test Conconi and its application. He was a member of the medical team for the 1980, 1984, and 1988 Olympic Games. Currently he is an adviser to the Medical Commission of the International Olympic Committee (IOC) and a scientific consultant for the Italian Olympic committee.

Conconi is married to Elisa Calzolari, a physician and geneticist. They live in Ferrara with their four children: Maria, Paola, Anna, and Michele.

Translator Patricia Ennis and author Francesco Conconi.

Journalist Patricia Ennis has been writing about cycling since 1982 and has published articles in *Velo-news, Winning, Bicycle Guide, Cyclist, Cycling USA,* and *Women's Sports and Fitness.* Since relocating to Italy in 1989, she has concentrated on European professional racing and has published interviews with Francesco Moser, Moreno Argentin, and Guido Bontempi.

This is her second book in translation. The first, authored by Italian journalist Gianni Brera, deals with the life and career of inventor and industrialist Tullio Campagnolo, founder of the Campagnolo bicycle components company.

Ennis first met Francesco Conconi in 1984, when she began reporting on his heart rate test and his work with Francesco Moser. Along with biomedical engineer Michael

Argentieri and computer programmer Linda Piper, Ennis conducted independent research on methods of performing the Test Conconi on windload trainers. The results of this research were published in *Velo-news* (July 12, 1985), *Bike Tech* (June 1987), and 'Medical and Scientific Aspects of Cycling,' edited by Edmund R. Burke and Mary M. Newsom (Champaign,IL: Human Kinetics Books, 1988).

Born in Camden, NJ, in 1950, Ennis graduated from Douglass College in 1972 with a degree in English literature. She did postgraduate studies in journalism at the University of California, Berkeley, and at Temple University in Philadelphia, PA.

Since discovering cycling in 1978, Ennis has been an avid rider, racer, and bicycle tour guide. She and her husband, an Italian cyclist, own a bike store near their home in northeastern Italy.